Bo

A Quarterback's
Journey Through
An SEC Season

BILLY WATKINS

The Nautilus Publishing Company
OXFORD, MISSISSIPPI

Bo: A Quarterback's Journey Through an SEC Season © copyright, 2015, by Billy Watkins. No part of this book may be reproduced without the express, written consent of the publisher except in the case of brief quotations embodied in critical articles and reviews.

For information, contact Nautilus Publishing, 426 S. Lamar Blvd., Oxford, MS 38655

ISBN: 978-1-936946-49-5

First Edition

Front cover design by Connor Covert. Front cover photo by Bruce Newman

Photo credits: Chapter 1: Getty Images; Chapter 5: Getty Images; Chapter 6: The Wallace Family; Chapter 9: The Wallace Family; Chapter 23: Bruce Newman; Chapter 24: Bruce Newman; Chapter 25: Getty Images; Chapter 28: Getty Images; Chapter 29: Getty Images; Chapter 30: Bruce Newman; Chapter 32: Getty Images

Library of Congress Cataloging-in-Publication Data has been applied for.
Printed in Canada

10   9   8   7   6   5   4   3   2   1

For Jimmy

Prologue

Everyone has an opinion of Bo Wallace.

Most of the time you don't even have to ask for it. Just mention his name and listen.

And only those who have paid close attention to his career — one that saw him win as many games (24) at quarterback for the Ole Miss Rebels as Eli Manning — are not likely to use the word "interception" in the first sentence.

It's as if he is the first quarterback to throw a football that was caught by the other team.

In his three seasons at Ole Miss, Bo Wallace threw 41 interceptions. Some of them were in the *why would he throw it there?* department.

Some were in the *why would he throw it there again?* department. I get that.

But I also remember what Bear Bryant always said when he was asked during postgame press conferences about plays he had called or personnel decisions he had made.

"I was trying to win the game," he would say.

If some poor scribe attempted a follow-up question, Bryant offered the same answer . . . only louder.

That's what I say when people ask me how Bo could have thrown 41 interceptions in 39 starts.

He was trying to win games.

He was trying as hard as anyone I've ever known. Many of his former

Ole Miss teammates agree.

"Obviously, every player in our locker room wanted to win," said Andrew Ritter, a placekicker and Bo's teammate in 2012 and 2013. "But there was nobody on our team who wanted to win as much as Bo did. He took losing personally. And I think every player respected him for that. I know I did."

And let's compare those 41 interceptions to others who came before him.

Auburn's Pat Sullivan threw 41 in his three-year career and won the Heisman Trophy.

At Ole Miss, Kent Austin threw 31 touchdowns, 41 interceptions.

Romaro Miller? 48 touchdowns; 34 interceptions.

Archie Manning? 31 touchdowns, 40 interceptions.

And the only quarterback to guide Ole Miss to a perfect season, Glynn Griffing in 1962, threw 11 touchdowns and 10 interceptions.

Bo finished with 62 touchdown passes to go with the 41 picks. Only Eli Manning has thrown more TD passes at Ole Miss.

He never missed a start. He never made an excuse. He never dodged the press. He played through pain and injuries. Most would have quit and watched from the sideline.

Football fans can only wish there was a stat for that.

· · ·

In the fourth game of his sophomore year, in the Superdome, while playing Tulane, Bo suffered a partially separated right shoulder. Yes, his throwing shoulder.

Four games later, before driving Ole Miss to a last-second winning field goal against Arkansas, he was hit on the shoulder again. This time the damage was worse.

He started the final four regular season games and the bowl game. He threw five touchdown passes in the Egg Bowl and helped make Ole Miss bowl-eligible in Hugh Freeze's first year as head coach. He threw three touchdowns in the BBVA Compass Bowl and earned Most Valuable Player honors. He also won the Conerly Trophy — awarded to the top college football player in Mississippi — that season.

The week following the bowl game, Bo traveled to Jackson, Mississippi, to the University of Mississippi Medical Center in Jackson. There, Dr. William Geissler performed the surgery. Geissler had been repairing shoulders since 1992 — the year Bo was born.

"Bo had the worst shoulder separation I've ever seen," Geissler said. "I don't know how he played in the SEC with it."

Geissler added, "He never complained. Not once."

I asked Geissler, who has been a part of Ole Miss' medical team for the past decade, *if 10 quarterbacks had this same injury how many would play through it?*

He thought for a moment.

"Bo might be about the only one," he said. Then, he added, "At least of the ones I've known. He is one tough guy."

While Bo's shoulder improved, it never returned to where it was before the injury.

Fans will recall Bo driving the Rebels down the field against sixth-ranked LSU his junior season and Ritter kicking a 41-yard field goal with 2 seconds left to win, 27-24.

Some might remember Bo running for two first downs on the drive, or the third-down pass to Ja-Mes Logan for another first down.

I will remember that he had a knot the size of a softball on his shoulder, He threw for 346 yards that night.

Inflammation from the injury and surgery made it almost impossible for him to lift his arm after the comeback victory.

. . .

Robert Ratliff was a backup quarterback and a teammate of Bo's in 2012 and 2013. He was a graduate assistant during the 2014 season.

"I've played a lot of sports with a lot of people," Ratliff said. "Bo has this unbelievable mindset and sense of resilience. And he's an unbelievable competitor. He doesn't listen to the naysayers, and that's incredibly difficult at this level.

"I was with him every day for three years. I respect him so much. He talked to everybody. He gave everybody the time of day, which is not always the case when you're the star and the starting quarterback. *Is Bo rough around the edges?* Yeah. And on television, that came across the wrong way sometimes. But he has a great heart. Anybody who doesn't like Bo Wallace hasn't had the chance — or taken the time — to get to know him."

Will Gleeson came to Ole Miss in 2013 as a punter from Australia. "One of the first things I noticed was that Bo has a certain aura around him. It's a rare thing. But he was a great teammate. If you wore the same color jersey he did, he supported you all the way."

Chuck Rounsaville, who has spent four decades covering Ole Miss sports for *The Spirit*, said, "Bo had no fear — of success, of failure, of the gravity of the moment, of putting everything on the line at all times. It's the way he competed that made him an unforgettable Ole Miss Rebel and one of my favorites of all time."

• • •

Bo grew up in Pulaski, Tennessee. He came from a working-class family.

He won a state championship in high school, a junior college national championship at East Mississippi Community College, and he won at Ole Miss.

He signed with the Rebels when the program was in shambles. Ole Miss had just finished a 2-10 season, and approximately 30 players — maybe more — were in danger of flunking out of school. He had other options. Mississippi State and Baylor wanted him.

"For some reason, the 2-win season and all the academic problems that were going on [under Houston Nutt] ... none of that fazed me," Bo said.

He chose to sign with Ole Miss and with new coach Hugh Freeze.

He led Ole Miss to a 7-6 record as a sophomore. That season laid the groundwork for Freeze and his staff to sign the highly regarded 2013 recruiting class.

"I love Bo," Freeze said, sitting in his office on the Ole Miss campus in early March, 2015.

"I don't have the success, my wife and kids don't have the life we have, these 32 staff members in here don't have the life they have and the raises they've had ... we don't have all of that without the success Bo helped bring. And I don't take that lightly."

Gary Danielson played quarterback in the National Football League for 13 seasons. During the past nine years, he has been the analyst on CBS' primary broadcast team that calls the featured SEC football game each week.

"Bo's place in Ole Miss football history potentially could be as important as any of the great players who have come through that program," Danielson said. "Coach Freeze had to have Bo to turn the program around. He was the perfect guy to bridge where they were to where they wanted to go.

"Did he have some warts? Yes. But I don't think they needed a guy who was a fancy runner. They needed a tough guy who would take the lumps and all the pressure of the job. When he took over, he's all they had. And everybody had less pressure, even Hugh Freeze, because a lot of criticism was directed at Bo. A lesser person would've crumbled under the scrutiny, the physical pounding, the competition week after week after week. Bo was a convenient excuse when things went wrong. I have total respect for the guy."

Danielson chuckled. "To me, Bo was like the guy who used to go on the old *Ed Sullivan Show* and spin plates. He would spin a plate, and they'd give him another one. Six plates. Seven plates. Eight. Well, eventually they fall and break, and everybody looks at him and goes 'What the hell are you doing?' That's about what Bo was asked to do. He had to spin eight plates at a time.

"I'll tell you this: Tim Tebow couldn't have done at Ole Miss what Bo did. Tebow didn't throw well enough."

. . .

This is how I came to know Bo.

He played at East Mississippi Community College.

It is one of my alma maters.

We talked for a while after his first spring game. We talked when I happened to run into him after games. I liked him. He was my kind of guy.

When the 2013 Egg Bowl played out — with Bo walking off Scott Field the goat of the game, I said to my youngest son: "He is going to have one long off season."

A voice in the back of my head said, "You're going to write about it."

I called Bo a couple of weeks later.

"Here's what I would like to do … " I said. I explained the concept for what turned out to be this book.

Without hesitation, Bo said, "I'm in."

He understood that while I was writing about him, this was *my* book. He was never promised a dime from it. To this day, we have never discussed money.

I wanted to tell his story. He wanted his story told.

When Bo and I visited in July, before the start of his senior season, I said, "The season is a grind, I understand that. There will be days and weeks when you are sick of your teammates, your coaches, the beat writers. And you'll be sick of me. There will be weeks when you don't want to talk, but … "

He interrupted me. Bo shook his head and said, "Nope. I'll talk to you every week."

Bo Wallace is a man of his word . . . as you'll see.

Billy Watkins
August 2, 2015

Chapter 1

November 28, 2013, Egg Bowl, Starkville

It was the perfect call: *14 Stutter*, a designed keep off right tackle.

As soon as Bo saw Mississippi State's defense shift to his left, where two receivers were spread wide, he knew there could be a clear path to the end zone, a little more than 11 yards away. A fake to running back Jaylen Walton racing left forced the linebackers to pause, creating ideal blocking angles for the right side of the Rebels' line.

He ran untouched to the 6, then veered left a couple of steps to avoid senior safety Niko Whitley, who appeared to have over pursued the play.

But just as Bo moved inside the 4, Whitley made a desperate lunge and swatted the football loose. It ricocheted off Bo's abdomen, then off his left arm and landed a yard deep in the end zone. It bounced three times before landing in the hands of defensive back Jamerson Love.

In overtime: State 17, Ole Miss 10.

A 3-point underdog and forced to start a true freshman at quarterback, State had become bowl eligible at 6-6. For the Rebels, 7-5, it was their second Southeastern Conference loss in a span of six days, and they had now dropped four of the past five Egg Bowls.

Davis-Wade Stadium turned jet engine loud as many of the 55,113 in

Bo Wallace on the last play of the 2013 Egg Bowl

attendance rang their cowbells as hard as they could. In the end zone, face down and not moving, lay Bo Wallace — the player State fans loved to hate the most.

MSU supporters that somehow gained sideline access during the game and those in the stands near Ole Miss' bench had already enjoyed giving the quarterback an earful after he threw three first-half interceptions. But Santa Claus couldn't have given them a better gift than beating their rival with Bo Wallace fumbling near the goal line in overtime.

"*Get up!!!!*" a voice inside Bo's head screamed. *"You're on national television! Don't let people across the country see you with your face in the dirt!"*

As Bo attempted to push himself off the ground, Whitley swooped in from behind, straddled the quarterback, and head-butted him back to the turf. State fans would later refer to it as nothing more than a heat-of-the-moment tap on the head. Ole Miss fans called it the ultimate cheap shot. Bo paid it little attention. He figured a State player had accidentally bumped him while running to celebrate with his teammates.

He slowly rose to his feet and began the long walk to the cramped visitors' locker room, located behind the end zone on the other end of the field.

His senses turned screwy. Fans wearing maroon yelled and pointed in his face, yet he heard nothing. Everything appeared to be happening in slow motion. Ole Miss graduate assistant coach Ryan Trevathan helped escort him through the maze. Once inside, Bo walked to his locker, grabbed his cell phone and deleted all of his social media apps.

He quickly texted his dad, who was walking out of the stadium: "This is the worst thing that could ever happen to me."

Bill Wallace was his usual old-school self. "We can only hope so," he replied.

Barry Brunetti, a senior and Bo's primary competitor for the starting quarterback position the past two seasons, was the first to hug him. They had never been particularly close but there was a mutual respect between them.

"We'll get through this together," Brunetti told him quietly.

Both quarterbacks joined their teammates around head coach Hugh Freeze. The second-year coach said:

"Everybody touch somebody, men. Hey, the only thing that will get you through difficult times in life is love, man. And faith. Love and faith. I don't understand everything. We didn't play our best game, obviously. We can't turn the ball over as many times as we did and expect to win. Defense, you played your guts out, man. Played your guts out."

Offensive line coach Matt Luke fought back tears as he urged Bo to keep his head up and reminded him that a game is never decided by one play. Senior backup quarterback Robert Ratliff hugged Bo and said: "I know you. You are about to have the greatest off-season and season of your life."

Meanwhile, Freeze was facing the media. He didn't mask his frustration. Yes, the Rebel defense held State to 296 total yards, but the offense managed only 318 yards and did not score a touchdown. Ole Miss' points came on a punt block and recovery in the end zone during the final seconds of the first half, the extra-point and a third-quarter field goal. Throw in the 24-10 loss to Missouri the previous Saturday, and Freeze's offense had scored one touchdown in its last eight quarters, plus one overtime. In Freeze's version of the no-huddle spread, Ole Miss had been averaging 34.5 points per game just two weeks earlier.

FREEZE: (opening statement) "Hard to talk about things after this game because it's so emotional and means so much to both fan bases. It's always difficult when you lose games, but when you lose your rival game at the end of the year and you had your chances to put it away, or make it a two-score game several times and didn't get it done, it's very difficult."
MEDIA: "Comment on Bo's night. What was going on with him?"
FREEZE: "I certainly never want to talk negatively about one of our kids, but anybody who watched the game knows he didn't have his best game. In this league, if you turn it over the number of times that we did, it's going to be difficult to win games."

MEDIA: "On Bo's interceptions in the first half, it seemed like he was trying to make a play when it wasn't one there."
FREEZE: (nodding) "Yeah. Bad decisions. Totally."

In the locker room, assistant athletic director for media relations Kyle Campbell asked Bo: "You ready to do this?" Meaning face the press.

"Yep, let's do it," he said.

Bo thought, "There is no way I'm going to be the punk quarterback who lost the game and then hid in the dressing room afterward."

He soon found himself standing just outside the dressing room with more than a dozen cameras and tape recorders aimed his way. His long hair was still wet from a quick shower. Bo and the media had to speak over the relentless clanging of cowbells by Bulldog fans that stayed around to celebrate.

MEDIA: "Can you tell us what happened on the fumble?"
BO: "I relaxed, I guess. I don't know. It opened up and I saw it, made a cut, and thought I was in there.
(shakes his head) Craziest thing that's ever happened to me."
MEDIA: "It's an obvious question, but what does it feel like at that moment?"
BO: (shakes his head again) "It's a feeling I've never felt before, man, … like your heart's been ripped out. Especially in this game."
MEDIA: "Offensively, y'all struggled … "
BO: "We were awful. Terrible. We're a lot better than we showed tonight, I know that. It's really frustrating."
MEDIA: "Seems like it's been lately, though (sic), that's one touchdown in two games."
BO: "Yeah. Like I said, it's frustrating. We've got to go in and get to work and come out in our bowl game and put up some numbers and put up some points."
MEDIA: "Coach Freeze said he felt like the interceptions were because of bad decisions. Do you feel that way?"
BO: "A tipped ball. That's gonna happen. A ball floated on me. That's one bad decision. He can say what he wants. That's one bad decision. The rest is just football. That kind of stuff

happens."

MEDIA: "You've been real good at protecting the ball. Was something different tonight?"

BO: "Naw, like I said, the first one sailed on me. I usually make that throw. I make that throw every day. It was one bad decision, he can say what he wants."

MEDIA: "What kind of effect does a lack of a running game have on things?"

BO: "It's tough, but at the same time I'm involved in that. I've got to get myself going, and I didn't really do that much tonight."

MEDIA: "Did you have any lingering effects from being sick?"

BO: (shaking his head as the question was asked) "Naw."

Bo despised any player who made excuses after a loss, and he wasn't about to play the flu card standing in Starkville.

But most folks, including many of his teammates, didn't have a clue how sick he was. "It doesn't mean we would've won the game if I'd been healthy," Bo said. "Give them credit. State did a good job on defense. They ran a scheme they hadn't shown all year, and we had a hard time getting a handle on it. They would show blitz from one side, and then come from the other. I had a hard time seeing it. Maybe being sick had something to do with that, I don't know."

• • •

Five days earlier, Bo began feeling achy at the team hotel in Tupelo the night before facing Missouri. His fever climbed to 102. "They gave me a Tamiflu shot, and I didn't go to any of the game-day meetings," he said.

Trina texted Bo a few hours before the game and asked if he was going to be able to play. Bo texted back, "Well, duh!"

On a brutally cold evening by Deep South standards — temperatures near freezing and a 17 mph north wind — Bo started and played most of the game. But ESPN sideline reporter Holly Rowe noticed in the first half that he "doesn't seem himself … he appears disoriented at times." Freeze

6 Bo: A Quarterback's Journey

confirmed to Rowe at halftime Bo was fighting a bug. "He looked glassy eyed," Freeze said postgame, "but he wanted to play and compete."

Bo completed 26 of 42 passes for 244 yards, and he threw one interception. Star receiver Donte Moncrief dropped a touchdown pass in the fourth quarter that would have pulled Ole Miss within one score.

"I don't remember much about the Missouri game," Bo said. "I felt terrible."

He felt a little better Sunday and Monday, but on Tuesday "it was hard to get through practice," he said. He was worse Wednesday, the eve of the Egg Bowl.

"The day before a game, I hydrate by slamming purple and orange Gatorades," he said. "But the antibiotics they'd given me caused me to get ulcers in my mouth. Gatorade burned so bad when I tried to drink it ... there was no way. I couldn't eat anything because my mouth was so sore, and that's really what had me feeling weak.

"By the middle of the third quarter I was cramping and felt like I was freezing to death."

He made it through the game on adrenaline and willpower, but as he boarded the team bus after the game his legs were wobbly from exhaustion and he was fuming about Freeze's comments that all three picks were due to "bad decisions." He heard that constantly in 2012 when his touchdowns-to-interceptions ratio was 22 to 17. He worked hard prior to the 2013 season on throwing the ball away instead of forcing passes into coverage, and he'd tossed 17 touchdowns and just six interceptions entering the Missouri game.

"The worst thing anybody could tell me after my sophomore year was that I'd made a 'bad decision.' (Freeze's) comments pissed me off because they weren't accurate," Bo said.

He stewed over it all the way back to Oxford, hood up, earphones on and his iPod pumping everything from hip-hop to country music. His parents and his siblings — sister Baylee, 18, and brother Bryce, 13, at the time — were waiting for him at his apartment. He was going to ride home with them for a delayed Thanksgiving get-together on Saturday in Pulaski.

"I've never seen him that down," Trina said.

As he packed a few things, Bo talked with his roommates — linebacker Denzel Nkemdiche and defensive back Chief Brown, both sophomores.

"We all knew what was coming in the days ahead," Bo said. "People were going to rip me and the team on the message boards and Twitter and the call-in shows. Chief and Denzel were like, 'Hey, we've got your back.' And we talked about how important it was for the team to stick together and not listen to all the criticism. We're SEC football players, so we knew the next two or three weeks were going to be rough."

Bo soon learned the criticism had started long before the game was over, and it wasn't aimed at any of the players. Baylee was angered by Freeze's halftime comments made to TV and radio reporters about how poorly Bo had performed.

She tweeted: *"Coach Freeze has absolutely no faith in Bo, don't think he has ever said anything good about him."*

Fans and the media jumped on it. Bo was furious with his sister.

They arrived in Pulaski around 4 a.m. and Bo finally fell asleep a couple of hours later. The fumble played over and over in his mind. He had no desire to see an actual replay.

A call to his cell phone awakened him shortly before 11 o'clock. He was surprised by the name on the screen.

Coach Freeze.

• • •

"I just wanted to make sure you're OK," Freeze said, the tone of his voice sounding more like the father of three daughters than an SEC football coach. Of course, he was both.

"I will be," Bo responded. "How are you doing?"

Freeze said he was sick about the loss and concerned about his quarterback. He invited Bo to lunch.

"I'm at home in Tennessee. We're having our Thanksgiving meal tomorrow."

"Oh, OK," Freeze said. "Well, I just wanted to talk with you and give you a heads up ... "

In a move rarely seen from a major college football coach, Freeze was about to release a statement addressing what was said at the postgame press conferences. Freeze wanted to be sure Bo was onboard with it before the statement was emailed to the media.

The statement read:

"After a disheartening and disappointing loss last night to Mississippi State, there were some quotes made by me and Bo Wallace that left the impression that I was too harsh on my evaluation of his play and some things he said sounded as if there is dissension between the two of us.

"First, I was asked a direct question about Bo's performance and gave what I thought was a legitimate answer. I probably shouldn't have said, in the heat of the moment and in the midst of the discouragement, that the turnovers were totally bad decisions. There was a tipped ball for one, a bad decision on another and a bad throw on one.

"Bo and I had a talk this morning and we are on the same page, both with his performance and in moving forward and where we are in the building of this program. His last words to me on the phone were that he was going to work his tail off to be the best quarterback in the SEC in our bowl game and next year.

"He is as disappointed with last night as I am, but we have to move forward, correct our mistakes and keep climbing. We have a lot of work to do from every angle and we can't get that done dwelling on something we can't change. We will analyze it, fix it, and give Rebel Nation everything we have to make sure games like that do not happen again. The game last night is not on Bo. I take full responsibility for the game last night. It is my job to have our players ready to perform at the highest level."

Bo told Freeze he agreed with every word. He thanked him for calling — and for supporting him publicly.

"It means a lot," Bo said.

"Look, you're my guy — good, bad, or indifferent," Freeze said. "I love you, and we're going to get past this, learn from it and be better because of it."

• • •

I interviewed Freeze and Bo separately about the "word war" in Starkville and their overall relationship. They would play the lead roles in determining Ole Miss' success or failure during the 2014 season, and the odds were good that at some point they would have another heat-of-the-moment clash. If I was going to write about Bo's senior journey through the SEC, I needed to have enough insight to distinguish a family squabble from a falling out. It was the only way I could be accurate.

"No one hurt for Bo Wallace more than I did after that game," Freeze said, sitting in his office at the Manning Center. "I was frustrated that it came across to some people that Freeze threw Bo under the bus ... I'm talking about at the post-game press conference. Bo knows I'll be straight with him.

"I wish like heck I had kept the text message he sent me after we hung up that morning [after the Egg Bowl]."

Bo said: "I sent him a text saying that I would work harder than ever in practice, that I would prepare harder than I ever had. It's not like I didn't prepare hard before, it's just that when you lose a game you look at everything under a microscope. I knew there were some things I could do better to prepare. I told him I'd work harder at being more vocal and the kind of leader it takes in a league like the SEC to win.

"Here's the deal: I get mad at Coach Freeze and he gets mad at me. But then we're over it. When I come to the sideline during a game and maybe something didn't go just right, he'll have his say, I'll have mine and then we move on. He allows me to say what's on my mind because he knows I'm competitive and I'm doing everything I can to win. I don't think any coach wants a quarterback who is afraid to express his opinion or offer a suggestion or tell him what I'm seeing out there. But I'm sure that comes across the wrong way sometimes on television. People think I'm being hard to deal with, not giving him proper respect. Freeze knows that's not the case.

"He is hard on me. Hard. Hard. Hard. But the truth is, I feel like I'm closer to him than anybody on the team. The public would never think that. But the fact that we have a history together makes our relationship unique. It's so unique everybody wants to figure it out. But nobody will ever figure it out except us. And that's all that really matters."

Chapter 2

Their paths crossed randomly, 155 miles northwest of the Ole Miss campus.

Bo signed with Arkansas State out of high school in 2010. Shortly after that, Freeze was named the Red Wolves' offensive coordinator.

It didn't take long for Bo to realize Arkansas State was not the place for him, and it had nothing to do with Freeze.

"I'm living in Jonesboro, Arkansas where I don't know anybody," Bo said. "I've just turned 18 years old and on my own for the first time. I get on campus and there are two quarterbacks ahead of me getting all the seven-on-seven snaps. That's a sobering thing for any quarterback that has always been the starter, always won.

"Every football player had an 8 o'clock class so they could be free in the afternoons for practice. Nobody wants an 8 o'clock class. I sure didn't. So I wouldn't go half the time and just hope that Freeze didn't find out. But he usually did. Every Sunday, I'm at the stadium doing up-downs and rolls till I'm puking."

Said Freeze: "I was just trying to teach Bo the meaning of accountability and buying into a team and a program and doing things the right way."

Meanwhile, Bo was watching sophomore quarterback Ryan Aplin throw for 2,934 yards and 21 touchdowns.

"Unless he broke both legs, Ryan was going to start for the next two years," Bo said. "I wasn't going to play if I stayed. I was miserable there. So I told my folks I was coming home."

Bill Wallace was firm with his son. "I told Bo if he came home, we'd have his stuff packed and waiting for him," he recalled. "I told him when he got to the house, to throw the keys to his truck on the kitchen table, and he'd have to find a job to support himself. I told him he'd have to buy a vehicle, pay the insurance on it.

"But I also told him if he'd wait until the end of the semester — and if he still wanted to transfer — we would try and work something out. I was trying to get him to see, 'Life ain't too bad there, son, if you look at the big picture.'"

Bo agreed to stay through that semester. "But he went into a deep depression and also came down with mononucleosis," Bill Wallace said. "He had a tough go of it there for a while. And I blame me and Trina for a lot of it. Bo was really young — barely 18 — and I don't think we'd prepared him to go off like that. We'd done everything for him. He was always busy playing ball. He didn't have to cut the grass at home. Hell, he didn't even have to cut up his breakfast — his mama did it for him. We just went a little too easy on him, and he was nowhere near ready to be living on his own."

Arkansas State finished 4-7. Bo informed Freeze and head coach Steve Roberts following the final game that he was transferring.

Freeze said too much has been made of their days at Arkansas State.

"Bo was a freshman. He's not the first freshman to do some irresponsible things," Freeze said. "Yeah, he made me mad at times, but there was never a time that I didn't want to coach him. And I understood his reason for transferring. He had a kid there in front of him who was going to play. Bo made the right decision for Bo."

It would prove to be a decision that, in time, would benefit Freeze as well.

• • •

Bo had decided to call UT-Martin and a couple of other schools over the Christmas holidays and see if they needed a quarterback.

David O'Conner, Bo's former coach at Giles County High School, got wind of Bo's plans and phoned Bill. "He's SEC material. That's where he needs to wind up. Let me make a call."

O'Conner knew a former assistant coach from Sparkman High School in Toney, Alabama who was the head coach at East Mississippi Community College in Scooba, Mississippi. Buddy Stephens ran a wide-open offense that O'Conner figured Bo would love. It would be another chance for recruiters to evaluate him, and if he could graduate in a year he would have three years of eligibility to play at a major college.

"I talked to Coach Stephens, told him about Bo, but he just wasn't sure," O'Conner said.

Stephens was recruiting Terrance Broadway, a dual-threat quarterback out of Baton Rouge who was looking to transfer after sitting his freshman season behind Case Keenum at the University of Houston where coach Kevin Sumlin's offenses were putting up video game type offensive numbers.

"I told Coach Stephens I would send him a tape," O'Conner said. "But I also told him, 'No matter what you see on there, you're not going to see his best qualities. Toughness. Competitiveness. Leadership.'"

Broadway committed to the University of Louisiana-Lafayette. Stephens soon traveled to the Wallace home in Pulaski.

"Coach Stephens was smart," Bo said, laughing. "He came to me. He didn't want me to see Scooba until I had signed. It's 45 minutes from the nearest mall."

While Scooba only has a population of approximately 700, folks drive from neighboring counties to cheer on the Lions. It is where Bob "Bull" Sullivan became a coaching legend. *Sports Illustrated* once ran a cover story by Frank DeFord about "the toughest coach there ever was." During practices, Sullivan would put his defensive linemen on the edge of a pond and challenge the offensive line to pile-drive them into the water. During blocking drills, Sullivan's players peeled the bark off mature pine trees instead of running into padded dummies. His teams wore helmets with a skull and crossbones insignia on both sides. They did not wear facemasks.

Sullivan stood 6-foot-4 and weighed 295 pounds. While there might have been a player or two through the years who could have whipped him in a fistfight, none was brave enough to try.

Even though Sullivan hadn't coached there since 1968, the love of junior college football he created in the area remained. EMCC was even opening a new $4.7 million, 5,000-seat stadium in 2011 — Sullivan-Windham Field where a 7-foot, 600 pound statue of Sullivan would be unveiled before the opening game.

Stephens liked what he saw on tape, liked Bo even more upon meeting him and his family. Bo signed with the Lions.

"That year at Scooba was one of the most fun years I've had," Bo said. "There were so many great athletes on that team. And everybody was trying to do enough to get a scholarship offer at the next level. In a lot of ways, it was the last chance most of us had to keep our careers going. And we all really came together. There were a lot of egos but we all wanted the same thing — to put on a show and win."

They did both.

EMCC went 12-0 on its way to the National Junior College Athletic Association national championship, scoring at least 45 points in eight games.

Running a scheme similar to Freeze's, Bo completed 336 of 502 passes (67 percent) for 4,604 yards and 53 touchdowns. He threw 14 interceptions, or one every 36 passes. His TD-to-interception ration was nearly 4-to-1. Bo set NJCAA records for yards passing and touchdown passes. He was named National Offensive Player of the Year, the first freshman to win the award since 2004.

On December 3, 2011, No. 2-ranked EMCC played No. 1-ranked Arizona Western in the NJCAA national championship game in Yuma, Arizona.

"I've never seen anything quite like I saw before that game," Bill Wallace said. "Arizona Western was acting kind of crazy during warm-ups … yelling at our players, strutting around, dancing. Our players had to go to the other end of the field to get to the dressing room. So when East Mississippi headed in after warm-ups, the Arizona Western players sort of formed a tunnel they had to run through, like you see Little League mamas do. I just knew a fight was going to break out any minute. Bo texted me after he got to the dressing room and said, 'We are fixing to put a butt-whipping on that bunch.'"

And they did, 55-47, to claim the national title. Bo completed 31 of 43 passes for 460 yards and seven touchdowns and was voted the game's Most Valuable Player on offense.

• • •

Two days after the championship game, at 7:45 a.m., the Ole Miss athletic department released a video. The title read: *A Message from Archie Manning*.

The legendary Rebel quarterback appeared seated in an executive office wearing a dark suit with a red and blue tie.

"Hi, I'm Archie Manning, co-chair of the search committee to find the next head football coach of the Ole Miss Rebels. Today is going to be a special day for the Ole Miss family."

Archie went on to thank Chancellor Dan Jones, his co-chair Mike Glenn and members of the committee.

"A lot of people know about Ole Miss and our tradition," Archie said, "and there was a lot of interest in this job.

"In addition to selecting a man of high character and integrity, the other criteria we used were the ability to build a staff, recruit this part of the country, develop these student-athletes, galvanize the fan base, and win the right way."

The screen faded briefly to black, and the camera moved to a close up of Archie. He smiled and said: "So after weeks of studying the candidates, many interviews, the decision was simple ... I am so excited to announce that Hugh Freeze is the next head football coach of the Ole Miss Rebels."

• • •

That same day, shortly after 2 p.m., Freeze was introduced to a packed house of media and fans at the Gertrude C. Ford Center on campus. It felt and sounded more like an old-fashioned tent revival than a press conference.

The 42-year-old Freeze had taken an interesting path to that stage.

He was born in Oxford and grew up an hour away on a dairy farm in Independence. His father, Danny, was an assistant high school football coach. Hugh Freeze became mesmerized by the game and its strategy at a young age.

After earning a math degree in 1992 from the University of Southern Mississippi, he was hired at Briarcrest Christian School in Memphis where he coached football and girls' basketball. He won two state football championships with Michael Oher, subject of the hit movie *The Blind Side*, playing left tackle. He served three seasons (2005-2007) at Ole Miss, the first as assistant athletic director for football external affairs and two as tight ends coach and recruiting coordinator, but was caught in the cross fire of the firing of head coach Ed Orgeron and his staff.

The Rebels won just 10 games in his three seasons in Oxford, but Ole Miss would be rewarded by his and Orgeron's recruiting efforts in 2008 and 2009 with two nine-win seasons and a pair of Cotton Bowl victories.

While Ole Miss was celebrating its first winning records since Eli Manning's senior season, Freeze was about as far from the limelight as a college coach can get. He took the job at tiny NAIA Lambuth College in Jackson, Tennessee and led the private Methodist school to 8-4 and 12-1 records. The 11-0 regular season record in 2009 was best in school history.

Arkansas State hired him as offensive coordinator in 2010 — the year he and Bo were together — and promoted him to head coach in 2011 when head coach Steve Roberts resigned. Freeze led Arkansas State to a 10-2 season and its first Sun Belt Conference title in six years. His fast-paced offense's 448 yards per game caught the committee's eye. Freeze sold them with his energy, his attention to detail and a genuine, infectious confidence.

So in the Ford Center, after thanking the Chancellor, Mike Glenn, and Archie, he became emotional as he turned to his family — wife, Jill, and their three daughters, Ragan, Jordan, and Madison.

"I've taken them all around the nation …"

His voice broke and trailed off. He paused and fought back tears. The crowd applauded.

"But I've taken them all around the nation to get back to one place, and that is *the* University of Mississippi."

The crowd roared.

He introduced his team's "its" — the self-identity traits for his staff and each unit.

"Offensively, to be a fundamentally efficient scoring machine," he said. "The defensive 'it' will be to relentlessly pursue the football and knock the ever-loving stink out of the opponent for sixty minutes. Our special teams 'it' will be to provide the winning edge. Our recruiting 'it' is to develop a dynamic relationship with the student athlete and every single person involved in the decision-making process."

He even challenged the fans. "The Rebel nation 'it' will simply be to unite as one."

"I understand where things are," he said. "I told our team today we are in the wilderness. And the plan I presented to the committee, it talks about 'the journey'. . . I understand the landscape of things. I understand your frustration. You give us a chance, we're going to win you over, we're going to win recruits and we're going to win football games because [the players] are tired of being in the wilderness . . . and it will start with attitude, how we talk to ourselves and what we believe about us."

"I promise you this: I will hire men that will change their lives. It may not always be the popular hire. They may not be the most popular experienced SEC guy. But ... the guys I will bring in here, they will impact these young men's lives and this program's attitude and we will become winners."

Near the end of his talk, Freeze introduced the program's new motto: *Win the day*. "Our daily actions have to meet our spoken goals," he said. "You can't say you want to be an honor roll student and not go to class. You can't say you want to be an All-American player and not practice hard every single day. *You have to win the day.*"

Chapter 3

Trina Wallace was the first in her family to mention a possible reunion of coach and quarterback.

"He's coming after you," Trina told Bo.

"No, Mom, he's not. Freeze thinks I'm a knucklehead," Bo said.

Bill Wallace agreed with Bo.

"OK. Y'all wait and see," Trina said.

Two things were certain: Bo played lights out at EMCC, and Freeze desperately needed a passing quarterback to run his up-tempo, spread offense. Ole Miss had three quarterbacks on its roster: seniors Randall Mackey and Zack Stoudt, and Brunetti, a junior who had transferred from West Virginia before his sophomore season and was rated the nation's No. 4 duel threat quarterback prospect coming out of Memphis University School. The three quarterbacks' combined passing stats in 2011 were not impressive: 1,815 yards, 9 touchdowns, 13 interceptions.

It seemed a cinch that Freeze would quickly offer, and Bo would commit.

"But I finally realized Ole Miss was 'slow playing' me," Bo said. "They were waiting to see what a couple of other quarterbacks were going to do."

The Rebels already had one quarterback committed — C.J. Beathard, a three-star prospect out of Franklin, Tenn. who would later change his mind and sign with Iowa.

But Freeze and staff were in hot pursuit of two in-state quarterbacks:

four-star Anthony Alford from Petal High School and four-star Jeremy Liggins from Lafayette County High School, just down the road from the Ole Miss campus.

At 295 pounds, Liggins was "probably going to eat his way out of being a quarterback," said one Mississippi high school coach. He predicted Liggins would end up a lineman or a tight end.

Alford was a Top 100 prospect, a four-star dual-threat quarterback who produced 3,789 yards of total offense and accounted for 44 touchdowns his senior season. Alford's three favorites: Ole Miss, LSU, and Southern Mississippi. Baseball scouts predicted Alford would be selected in the first few rounds of the Major League draft in June.

Bo visited Ole Miss in mid-December and told reporters afterward that he was "ready to go" if offered a scholarship. Days passed. The calendar turned to 2012. Bo's only offers were from Indiana, Middle Tennessee State, and the University of Alabama-Birmingham (UAB).

But he soon picked up another. Mississippi State offered, and head coach Dan Mullen visited with Bo and his parents at their home in Pulaski. He made a grand entrance, flying into the tiny airport nearby on the university's jet.

"He talked to me about coaching Alex Smith and Tim Tebow. He told me that he demands a lot out of his quarterbacks, but he said he thought I could handle it. He said I would battle (Tyler) Russell and Dak (Prescott) in the spring for the starting job. I have to give him credit. He did a good job recruiting me. And flying to Pulaski just to talk to me really impressed my parents."

Bo took four visits in four days, January 4th through the 7th : Indiana, MSU, Baylor, and (unofficially) Ole Miss.

"Kevin Wilson was the head coach at Indiana, and he had coached Sam Bradford at Oklahoma. Bradford was one of my favorite quarterbacks," Bo said. "Seth Littrell was going to be the offensive coordinator, and he was coming from Arizona where they really threw the ball around. I could see myself playing at Indiana."

Bo spent time in Starkville with MSU offensive coordinator Les Koenning. "I had been there once before. When I was at [EMCC], some of us went up for the State-Alabama game. I didn't really have a feel for the place one way or the other. Their offensive line coach [John Hevesty] was on the sidelines at our national championship game, I remember that." Hevesty was recruiting Bo and defensive end Demico Autry.

Baylor was trending. Its offense was consistently putting up outrageous numbers. Quarterback Robert Griffin III had just won the Heisman Trophy and was headed to the NFL. "I was with Coach [Art] Briles most of my day there. He really impressed me, and I knew they could develop me there."

At Ole Miss, Bo met with tight ends coach Maurice Harris and offensive line coach Matt Luke. Freeze hadn't hired an offensive coordinator/quarterbacks coach. "I had no idea who would be coaching me, but that was OK. I knew Freeze would be calling the plays."

With classes starting soon, Bo couldn't wait much longer to make a decision.

On January 7, Alford committed to Southern Mississippi. Bo was happy to hear it. Maybe now he might get a phone call from Oxford.

"My parents really wanted me to go to State. All they knew was, I wasn't happy at Arkansas State and Freeze was there. I think that worked against Coach Freeze with them. And they were all about Mullen."

Ole Miss fans were starting to squirm. Why wasn't Freeze offering Bo? A record-setting junior college quarterback with three years of eligibility remaining doesn't come along every year.

Finally, on January 9, news broke out of Oxford that Ole Miss had offered. Bo accepted the next day.

"I already knew Freeze's system. And I really wanted to play in the SEC. It was a good fit for me," he said. "I knew if I went to Ole Miss it would come down to me and Brunetti for the quarterback job. I called State and talked with Coach Koenning. He was nice about it. He said, 'Good luck to you. I just don't think that's the best decision for you.'

"Looking back, I can't imagine myself going anywhere else. To me, it worked out just like it was supposed to.

"There is something I've never really talked about. I remember emailing [then Ole Miss offensive coordinator] Kent Austin my senior year. I told him how much I wanted to be the quarterback at Ole Miss, that I loved their offense and that I could win for him. I never heard anything back. They had shown some interest in me my sophomore and junior year."

He visited Ole Miss on September 20, 2008 for the Vanderbilt game, which the Rebels lost 23-17. Dexter McCluster, the lightning quick running back, had not yet found his game-changing form and fumbled inside the 1-yard line in the final seconds. A week later, Ole Miss stunned No. 1 Florida and quarterback Tim Tebow, 31-30, at The Swamp in Gainesville. Bo watched that game on television.

"I remember hanging out a little bit with [defensive end] Carlos Thompson on my visit," Bo said. "And Ole Miss really impressed me because everybody knew who I was when I got there. But as the season went along, they just sort of went away. I didn't hear anything else from them.

"But I could never get that trip to Oxford out of my mind. My mom — who was Tennessee Volunteers through and through — was on the trip with me. She told me, 'I could see you coming to school here.' Turns out, she was right again."

• • •

It didn't take him long to learn that the quarterback position at Ole Miss is high profile and year-round.

Sixteen days after committing to Ole Miss, Bo was cited for under-aged drinking at Rooster's on Oxford's town square. He was 20.

"So you're the new quarterback, huh?" the police officer asked as he wrote the citation.

"Yes, sir."

The officer tore the ticket from his pad and handed it to Bo. "Get another one of these and you won't be."

Chapter 4

December 19, 2013

A few minutes past 4 p.m., Bo walked out of the Manning Center — Ole Miss' indoor practice facility named after Archie and Olivia Manning — wearing a blue t-shirt, blue sweatpants and flip-flops. He had just finished watching video of Georgia Tech, the Rebels' opponent in the Music City Bowl on December 30 in Nashville.

"They're probably middle of the road, compared to the defenses we've seen this season," he said.

Both teams finished the regular season 7-5. Las Vegas listed Ole Miss a 3-point favorite, but there was no brash talk coming from the locker room. Defensively, they were learning the discipline it takes to handle Georgia Tech's triple-option scheme. Offensively, the Rebels were stinging after two poor showings to end the regular season. Their swagger had taken a serious hit.

Sometimes a bowl game is more than a reward. It can be a second chance. That was how Freeze's players looked at their date with the Yellow Jackets as they departed campus for the holidays and prepared to gather in Nashville on Christmas Day.

Bo remained in Oxford a couple of extra days to study more tape and get treatment on his shoulder. Three weeks had passed since the nightmare finish in Starkville. The mental anguish hadn't eased up much.

"I can honestly say these have been three of the toughest weeks of my life," Bo said. "Losing a game like that to State ... it's still surreal to me."

On the Monday following the Egg Bowl, Bo had decided to skip his 8 a.m. class. He didn't want to deal with the stares or answer questions about the fumble or the loss. Even worse, he didn't want condolences or pep talks. He just wanted to get to Nashville and play the bowl game.

At 7:45, offensive coordinator Dan Werner called.

"Just wanted to make sure you'll be at your 8 o'clock class," he said.

"I probably wasn't going," Bo said, "but I guess I will now. I haven't missed one yet."

Yes, there were a few stares and a sprinkling of comments as he walked across campus and into the classroom.

"Tough game, man."

"Y'all still had a good year."

"I thought you'd scored."

But one comment stood out: *"We get State here next year. Make them pay."*

Yes, he was already thinking about next year's Egg Bowl. November 29, 2014. It would be his last game at Vaught-Hemingway Stadium. Senior Day. He couldn't imagine the emotion of walking out of the tunnel on game day for the final time. He thought of his mom.

"I know she'll be crying before the game," he said. "But she won't be crying after it because we're gonna beat the hell out of 'em. You can write that down."

There was a serious edge to his voice.

"I don't know, there was something missing those last two games. It wasn't just me being sick," he said. "Last year [2012], we went out and played hard as we could every week. Didn't matter who we were playing. We were so hungry to get to a bowl game. And then this year we were sitting there 7-3, and everybody is telling us we are going to finish 9-3 and going to this bowl or that bowl. And I'm not saying we didn't prepare and play hard, but some guys didn't have a lot of respect for Missouri because the East [division] seemed so average. They were talking like we were going to beat the brakes off of 'em, and I was like, 'OK. But they've only lost one game. They must be pretty good because wins in the SEC don't come easy.' And as it turned out, they were pretty good."

Two great opportunities wasted to end the 2013 regular season. He refused to waste another one, team-wise or personally.

"I've got to get back on a football field and redeem myself," he said. "And we don't have another game for eight months after this bowl, so we've got no choice but to win. I've got no choice but to play like I'm supposed to. It'll be good for us to get some momentum going into next year. And it'll be good for me.

"Look, I hear what's being said by the fans. People think maybe I shouldn't be the quarterback next year. They're saying Ryan or Devante will beat me out of the job. I just want to play well in the bowl game and shut folks up.

"But the one thing I can't do is go out there and try too hard. That's definitely something I've got to guard against. I think maybe against State, when things started going downhill, I started trying too hard, trying to make too many plays."

. . .

He also heard fans on radio call-in shows chiming in about his social life.

"Wow, that didn't take long. It's barely been a week and Bo Wallace is already out on the town. He must have taken that loss in Starkville really hard."

"Yeah, I was out," he said. "I had two junior college prospects with me — offensive linemen we were trying to sign. The coaches asked me to take them out, show them a good time. One has signed with us. Fahn Cooper."

Chapter 5

DECEMBER 30, 2013, MUSIC CITY BOWL

With Nashville only an hour north of Pulaski, this was like a home game for Bo. He went out only once, the night after Christmas. He took several teammates to some of his favorite hangouts, introduced them to friends he grew up with. After that, it became a business trip.

His intensity in practice was noticeable, his attention to detail impressive. Every bowl practice, he pushed his teammates to focus. He was more vocal than he'd ever been "which really isn't something Bo has been comfortable with," Freeze said. "But I can see him growing into that role of being a guy who will hold others accountable."

The night before the game, Bo sat in his hotel room and watched tapes of Georgia Tech's defense for the umpteenth time.

"I had a real feel for what they liked to do, how they tried to defend certain formations," he said. "I was really confident. I wasn't as worried as much about Tech as I was trying too hard to make plays. I really tried to clear my mind that night, get a good night's sleep. and be ready to roll the next day."

He received a text from Freeze before turning in.

It read: "Love the way you're preparing. Go have fun tomorrow. And be confident. I love you."

"That really meant a lot to me," Bo said.

• • •

Wearing their traditional home uniforms — navy blue helmets, red jerseys, gray pants — the Rebels looked hungry and sharp on the game's opening possession. Bo completed his first pass, 7 yards to Moncrief on third-and-6 to the Ole Miss 29. He threw to Jordan Holder for 5, to Moncrief for 11, to Cody Core for 5. Running back I'Tavius Mathers gained 15 yards on two carries.

Freeze gave his offense a confidence boost by choosing to go for it on fourth-and-5 at the Tech 28. Bo connected with running back Jaylen Walton for 6 yards and a first down. That helped set up a play straight from a movie script.

On third-and-5 from the Tech 17, Bo dropped back to pass, saw an opening in the middle and took off. He ran untouched to the 8, then cut left as the safety approached. Just before the defender reached to get a hand on him, Bo switched the ball from his right arm to his left — away from potential trouble. The safety lunged and only got a hand on Bo's leg. Touchdown.

Bo received a flying chest bump from wide receiver Quincy Adeboyejo, then trotted to the sideline. Freeze was waiting for him. They embraced. It was not lost on his teammates, either, that the play was eerily similar to the one in Starkville. They made a point of sharing a high-five or a pat on the shoulder pads with their quarterback. It was as if fate dealt him an immediate do-over.

"While I was running, I didn't have any kind of flashback or anything. I was just trying to get in the end zone," he said. "But I thought about it after I scored. I felt relief, to be honest. And it felt good to celebrate with my coach and teammates."

Bo would score again on a run with 8:13 left in the third quarter to put the Rebels ahead 20-7. He faked to Mathers going right and bolted up the middle 10 yards for a touchdown. He faked left at the 5, leaving the Tech safety flat-footed. The offensive line mobbed Bo in the end zone.

"That time I remember putting both hands over the ball when the safety came up," he said. "Just a fundamental thing I had worked on during practices leading up to the bowl.

"I kept telling myself, 'Don't try to be the hero. Make the plays when they're there, but don't force anything. If we have to punt, that's okay.' But we were able to make some plays because the offensive line played really well. Those guys took care of me."

Tech intercepted Bo once, an underthrown ball to Moncrief down the left sideline at the Tech 28 with 13:38 left and Ole Miss leading 23-10. The Yellow Jackets quickly made it 23-17 with a 72-yard touchdown pass.

Ole Miss' defense forced a safety on a reverse and fumble to make it 25-17 with 4:22 left. Still, Paul Johnson's gritty team was within one score and a two-point conversion. Ole Miss' offense had to at least gain some yards and run the clock.

It came down to a third-and-13 play at the Ole Miss 42 with just less than 2 minutes remaining. The safe call would have been to run the ball, take time off the clock and punt.

Instead, Freeze put the game in his quarterback's hands. Bo responded by standing in the pocket against pressure from the Tech front and threaded a 27-yard strike to wideout Laquon Treadwell, who was surrounded by three defenders.

Even though it was the game's seal-the-deal moment, the play didn't get a lot of postgame attention and wasn't included in some game stories by major outlets. No matter. It was a clutch throw and catch, and a heck of a way for Bo to go into the offseason.

"I couldn't get a lot on that ball to Laquon, but I got it where it needed to be," he said. "And it really wasn't my arm or my shoulder that was the problem. It was my core. Because I couldn't lift weights during the offseason after my surgery, my body started breaking down from the grind of the sea-

Bo after the 25-17 Music City Bowl victory over Georgia Tech

son. I can't wait to have a full offseason to lift weights with [strength coach] Paul Jackson and to feel like I used to.

"My form was so bad ... I don't want to watch tape of the game. I'm sure my throwing motion looks terrible. I have to drop my throwing shoulder to get any kind of zip on the ball. It can't look good. But, hey, I play different than most quarterbacks, anyway. I play kind of awkward. I know that. But the key is to be productive and win. That's all that matters."

Coordinator Dave Wommack's defense did its part. Tech entered the game with the fourth-best rushing attack in the nation, averaging 311 yards per game on the ground. The Rebels held them to 151. The Yellow Jackets gained 298 yards total, 72 coming on the touchdown pass when the Rebels' secondary inexplicably turned a receiver loose deep.

In his final game as a junior, Bo threw for 256 yards and one touchdown, a 28-yard crossing route to Moncrief, who caught 6 passes for 113 yards. Bo also led the team in rushing with 86 yards on 13 carries.

He surpassed Eli Manning's single-season records for total offense (3,701) and completions (283).

A strange stat: In consecutive bowls, Bo completed 22 of 32 passes (69 percent). His 44 of 64 passing totaled 407 yards with 4 touchdowns and 3 interceptions. He accounted for six touchdowns, and the Rebels averaged 31.5 points per bowl game. Most of all, they won both.

• • •

Freeze left no room for a misunderstanding when talking with the media postgame about the play of his quarterback.

"I'm so proud of Bo, obviously. I've said every time somebody would ask me that the quarterback in (the SEC) gets way too much of the criticism when things don't go your way. People have bad days at work. Bo has had a few.

"But there is no way we're sitting here with 15 wins in two years and two bowl victories had Bo not been with us."

Freeze didn't discuss it at the press conference, but he saw Bo deliver everything he had promised in his text the morning after the Egg Bowl.

"Bo played like a stallion," Freeze said later. "No question, he was a different guy the day of, and leading up to, the Music City Bowl. His whole approach to preparing was different. Studying film. He just seemed really into it.

"One thing I believe is that he finally realized, 'Hey, a lot of people are depending on me.'"

Bo agreed. "Even going into my junior year, I don't think I understood the magnitude of being the starting quarterback at Ole Miss.

"But I know one thing: I understand it now — and just in time for my senior year. Time has gone by so fast. I really want to try and enjoy every day, every moment from here on out. I want the 2014 season to be one to remember. Not just for me, but for my teammates, my coaches and the fans. And I think we have a chance to make that happen."

Chapter 6

Bo usually kept his pre-game chatting with family members to a simple text to his dad moments before taking the field.

"It would be 'We're ready for this,' or something along those lines," Bill Wallace said. "Sometimes I might text him back and say 'Don't try to do any more than the defense is giving you.' The same sort of stuff we might have said when he was a little kid and I was coaching him."

Bo loved sports before he was old enough to attend kindergarten.

"We're a sports family," Bill said. "Me and Trina are both sports fanatics, and we probably carry it to the extreme."

When they attended Atlanta Braves games, Bo would paint his face in the team's red and blue colors.

"I could recite their lineup for years when they had guys like Ryan Klesko, Walt Weiss, and Javier Lopez," he said. "My favorite player was Chipper Jones. My whole family loved Chipper."

He grew up a football fan of the Tennessee Volunteers and players such as Jamal Lewis, Travis Henry, Cedric Wilson. And, of course, Peyton Manning.

"When I worked the Manning camp, my mom would ask me, 'Can't you get a picture with you and Peyton together?' And I'm like, 'No, Mom, I'm not five years old anymore.'"

They were Tennessee Titans fans, too.

"I can remember we had an upstairs playroom, and half the room was devoted to the Titans and the other half to the Vols. The walls were painted in their colors. That was normal for us," Bo said.

Bill bought Bo a go-kart when he was three and cut a figure-eight track in the pasture.

"I fixed it up to fit him real good, cushioned the seats," Bill said. "He could drive the fire out of that thing when he was three."

Bill and Trina were NASCAR fans, and Dale Earnhardt was their favorite driver. He soon became Bo's favorite, too. The family attended the Daytona 500 three times when Bo was growing up.

They weren't there in 2001 when Earnhardt died in a crash on the final lap.

"That sort of did it for us and NASCAR," Bill said. "I don't think we've watched a race since. It just took the fun out of the whole thing."

. . .

Bo's first foray into team sports also occurred at age three: T-ball.

"You were supposed to be at least four," Trina recalls, "but we would take him to the games and they'd let him play. Most three-year-olds didn't know anything about ball, but Bo did. Bill was always working with him."

Bill Wallace had been a star running back at Richland High School, a Class A school located in the northern portion of Giles County.

"We didn't use a quarterback in the traditional way. We ran the Single Wing offense," said Ron Shirey, who was a coach on the Richland staff at the time. "It's a lot like the Shotgun is today. We put Bill at tailback, put an extra guard in to block and snapped it directly to Bill.

"He wasn't nearly as big as Bo, but he was strong. He had two brothers to play at Richland before him, Buster and Brian, and all three were country boys who loved to play ball back in the day.

"Bill was lightning quick. He could make people miss. And I don't ever remember anybody really getting a solid lick on him. He had great vision and could really accelerate through the hole."

Richland won 13 games Bill's senior year and reached the state championship game.

"We probably won a couple of playoff games we shouldn't have," Shirey said, "and we got our ears waxed in the championship game. But it was a great season for the school. Bill was up for Mr. Football. Of course, Bo was eventually up for it, too — and won it.

"It really is a fairy tale football story. The daddy is 'the guy' in Giles County. Then his son comes along and he's 'the guy' in Giles County. You just don't see that happen very often."

• • •

Bo played organized football for the first time in the fourth grade. He learned quickly that he loved the physical nature of it.

"I remember this team had a really good player who was a running back and a middle linebacker. This guy put fear in people. You were always kinda looking to see where he was," Bo said. "When I was running the ball one time, he came up and put his helmet square in my chest — right in the diaphragm. It knocked the breath out of me. And to this day, it hurts when you get the breath knocked out of you. But for some reason, it didn't bother me to get hit. And I loved dishing out the licks even more. It was just a natural thing inside me."

When Bo was in fifth-grade, his dad coached and had the 10- and 11-year-olds running a no-huddle, spread offense. Bo was the quarterback.

"We all had wristbands with three colors on it — red, green, and blue," Bo said. "And each wideout and running back would have different wrist bands to tell them what to do whenever I called out a color. If I yelled 'red!' one wideout's wrist band would say 'slant,' another one's would say 'takeoff.' We were hard to stop."

He played baseball and basketball, too.

"I was a pitcher, catcher, shortstop, and second baseman in baseball,

Bo, dreaming of his future

and my dad coached me through my 14-year-old season," he said. "We had a really good team when I was 12, so a bunch of us chose not to play football my sixth grade year and play fall baseball, instead. We were a traveling team, and we probably played 70 games that year."

He returned to football in the seventh grade on Richland's middle school squad. Bo played quarterback for two years. His eighth-grade team lost only once, and he threw five touchdown passes in the final game. "That was the year I started thinking that I might be able to do something in football some day if I stuck with it and worked at it," Bo said.

He went through high school basketball tryouts the summer before his ninth-grade year and earned a varsity jersey.

Even though it was Bill and Trina's alma mater and the only school Bo had ever attended, Richland was a 1A school and didn't offer the kind of competition needed for a player hoping for scholarship offers from big-time colleges. The Giles County High School Bobcats played at the Class 4A level, and Bill had heard good things about their new football coach, David O'Conner.

Students were permitted to transfer from Richland to Giles County without having to sit out a season because the schools in the county weren't zoned.

One problem: Richland and Giles County were furious rivals.

"They hated each other," Bill Wallace said bluntly. "And you have to understand, at that time Trina and I both bled orange — not for the Tennessee Vols, but for Richland. Their school colors are orange and black.

"Bo was the first one to mention anything about transferring. Back in Pop Warner ball, our Richland team played Giles County, and it was serious business. Bo's fifth-grade year, we beat them 16-8, and the Giles County folks were coming apart after that. It killed them to lose to us. And they were loaded with athletes. I just think maybe our players were coached a little better. Giles County kept on and on about playing again that year. We finally agreed to it, and they beat us something like 20-12.

"We beat them Bo's seventh grade year, beat them again Bo's eighth-grade year. But Bo wasn't blind. He could see that Giles County had a bunch of talent over there. So at some point during his eighth-grade year, Bo told me and Trina, 'I want to transfer.'"

Bo's parents had countless discussions about it. They wanted to do what was best for their son, but they also realized the fallout that was sure to come.

"We would look at each other and say, 'Are we really going to do this? Are we really going to leave Richland and go to *Giles County?*'

"I'll never forget the day I had to go to the Richland school and tell the principal we were transferring. She jumped out of her chair and said, 'Well, you're nothing but a traitor!'

"Richland was mad at us. And a lot of folks at Giles County weren't too happy about it, either. Bo was going to eventually take somebody's spot, and we were known as people who played for 'that other team.' It wasn't all kisses and hugs. It was probably his junior year before most people didn't look at us as 'outsiders.' And there were probably a few people who never accepted us. But winning cures a lot of things."

• • •

Even though he was inheriting a talented roster, O'Conner had plenty of work to do after accepting the job at Giles County prior to the 2006 season. The Bobcats hadn't experienced a winning record since 1999. O'Conner enjoyed such challenges, having coached Lee High of Huntsville, Alabama to the playoffs three times in his four seasons as head coach. *The Huntsville Times* named him its 2005 co-Coach of the Year following Lee's 10-3 season and a trip to the Class 5A quarterfinals.

O'Conner knew the value of a good quarterback, and he was confident enough to welcome the Wallace family with open arms. He wasn't interested in the Richland-Giles County feud or anything that had happened prior to his arrival.

"One of the hot topics when I got there was about a kid going to school up in the northern part of the county that was going to be really good," O'Conner recalled. "That spring, Bo's dad came over and said they were thinking about transferring. I didn't hear anything else.

"But then the first day of fall practice, Bo enrolls. He was already a little over six feet. He came out for practice, and I could tell he had a really strong arm for his age. I was impressed with how he carried himself, how he picked things up quicker than most kids."

O'Conner wasn't sure what to do with him. "We had a senior quarterback but nobody to back him up. We weren't sure whether to keep Bo with the varsity or let him play some junior varsity games. We decided to put him on the high school team, but he didn't play any the first three weeks of the season. So we decided to let him play a JV game."

While being horse-collar tackled, Bo suffered a broken right foot. Doctors said he would miss at least six weeks.

On crutches and in a protective boot, Bo continued attending practice. "He would stand back there and watch and study everything, learn all the routes on our pass plays," O'Conner said.

In the season's seventh game, Giles County's starting quarterback suffered a knee injury and was out indefinitely.

As soon as he got home after the game, Bo started lobbying his dad to get him out of the boot so he could start for the 7-0 Bobcats the next week.

Said Bill: "I've had the same family doctor forever. He's been our kids' doctor. That Monday, we took Bo to him and told him the situation. He took an X-Ray of Bo's foot, looked at it and said, 'It looks pretty good.' But the orthopedic doctor we had been to would have to sign off on it. So we went to him. He looked at it and gave us the go-ahead."

"Bo comes to me that Monday afternoon and says, 'Coach, I can play. I can get this boot off. My daddy and the doctor have already told me I can,'" O'Conner said. "I'm standing there listening to him, but I'm not so sure he should be getting out of the boot a week early. But Bo was determined he was going to play. He got the boot off Wednesday, practiced Thursday and started on Friday night."

Bo couldn't have picked a much tougher opponent for his high school debut — and on the road, too. David Lipscomb Academy of Nashville was on its way to the Class 4A state championship game. They were consistently well coached and stocked with good players.

Lipscomb beat the Bobcats, 28-3.

"They brought all kind of blitzes, reminded him that he was a freshman," O'Conner said.

But the next week, in a 27-7 win over Creek Wood, Bo completed 10 of 18 passes for 180 yards and two touchdowns.

The senior would return for the final four games — three regular-season wins and another loss to Lipscomb, 21-14, in the first round of the playoffs.

"The improvement was clear to anybody who watched Giles County play," Bill Wallace said. "No coach had ever come in there and worked them boys like O'Conner did. I knew we were fixing to be pretty good."

Chapter 7

As a sophomore, Bo had the best group of receivers he would throw to at Giles County.

"We didn't run a lot of screens and short stuff," O'Conner said. "Most of our plays called for throws in the 12- to 16-yard range."

The Bobcats opened with an 18-10 overtime win over Humboldt. Bo scored the winning touchdown on a 4-yard run and completed 15 of 23 passes for 231 yards.

A week later, they held on for a 14-13 victory over another rival, Lawrence County, after leading 14-0 in the first quarter. Bo was 8 of 12 passing for 111 yards but tossed two interceptions.

Bo had a break-through game the next week, throwing for 299 yards and four touchdowns in a 66-20 victory over Cheatham County.

Giles County moved to 4-0 with a 41-16 win at Spring Hill. Bo was 7 of 10 passing for 87 yards, two touchdowns, two picks. He rushed 8 times for 63 yards.

But the Bobcats stumbled at home against Columbia Central in Week 5, losing 26-7. Bo had one of his worst games at Giles County: 5 of 17 passing, 119 yards, no touchdowns, two interceptions. He rushed 12 times for 51 yards.

"We reminded ourselves that Bo was still a sophomore, still learning.

And we were 4-1, so we felt good about things," O'Conner said.

Giles County bounced back to win consecutive road games, 63-0 over winless Montgomery Central and 35-14 at Page. In those games, Bo was a combined 16 of 30 for 313 yards, four touchdowns no interceptions.

And then came Lipscomb, which would go on to claim the Class 3A state championship.

The Mustangs rushed for 259 yards and four touchdowns in a 35-3 rout. Giles County managed just 233 yards total offense. Bo completed 5 of 10 passes for 67 yards and threw one interception.

"Right before halftime, Bo comes to the sideline during a time out," O'-Conner said. "He had just gotten the crap knocked out of him. I mean, *lit up!* He goes, 'Coach, I might need to come out one play.' I look at him and say, 'And who do you suggest we put in at quarterback?' Point being, we didn't have anybody.

"So he goes back in. We break the huddle, and Bo proceeds to line up behind the guard. The center doesn't realize it and snaps the ball. It goes sailing over our running back's head. One of their defensive ends scoops it up and runs it down there close. They score right after that, and now instead of 14-3, it's 21-3.

"After the kickoff, Bo didn't give me the chance to put anybody in. He goes running out there. Finishes the half. Finishes the game. Looking back, I'm pretty sure he had a concussion and I shouldn't have let him go back in. Today, I know I wouldn't. But once again, that's Bo Wallace for you. If he's breathing, he's going to play."

Bo played the best game of his sophomore season the next week, a 38-15 drubbing of Creek Wood. He threw for 323 yards, five touchdowns, and zero interceptions. Giles County stood 7-2 with one regular season game left, plus the playoffs.

But real life was about to rattle the Wallace family to its core.

• • •

Trina Wallace noticed that she had to catch her breath after walking up the bleachers at Bo's games. She had lost weight, too. Several people had mentioned it.

Trina, who stands 5-foot-7 and has never come close to being considered overweight, chalked it up to the stress of her job.

For 18 years, after graduating from Richland High School in 1987, Trina worked for Rackley Systems, which installs security systems in homes and businesses. She and a co-worker decided to quit in 2005 and open Sports Zone, a sporting goods store.

"When you're starting a business, you have a lot of responsibility pile up on you," she said. "I noticed a difference in everything about me. I was depressed … and I had this constant, hacking cough."

She got out of Sports Zone and started a new job on Halloween 2007, two days before Giles County played its regular-season finale at Marshall County.

"I was really hurting," she said. "My side was killing me and thought I must have pneumonia. I told my boss about 3:30 that afternoon, 'I know this is my first day, but I need to leave early and go the doctor.' "

Trina called no family members or friends. She sat alone for nearly two hours in the waiting room of Dr. Charles Haney.

"Dr. Haney had been my doctor since I was a child, and he joked that the only time I came to see him was to get a pregnancy test or if I had back trouble," she said. "I told him what was going on. He listened to my heart and couldn't believe how fast it was beating. He asked me if I was taking diet pills, which would explain the rapid heart rate and the weight loss."

He ordered a chest X-Ray, which revealed a mass so large her heart wasn't visible.

"He said, 'I don't know what it is, but it's serious,' " Trina said. "He made me an appointment to get a CAT scan the next morning. By now, it was nearly 8 o'clock and I was devastated. I had to try and figure a way to tell Bill without the children finding out."

She couldn't sleep that night. Bill drove her to get the CAT scan the next day, then to an appointment with an oncologist 90 minutes away in Murfreesboro. Dr. Victor Gian informed Trina: "I'm pretty sure you have lymphoma, but let's wait and see what the biopsy says tomorrow."

Indeed, she was diagnosed with Hodgkin's Lymphoma on a Friday morning — game day for Giles County.

Hodgkin's lymphoma is a cancer that attacks the lymph tissue, which is found in the lymph nodes, bone marrow, spleen, liver, and other areas. It is among the most curable cancers — but not without a serious fight. Trina would require 12 rounds of chemotherapy, one every other week.

"We're talking about six or seven months of chemo, so there was no way to do it without telling the kids," she said. "Bo was fixing to go to the playoffs, and there was no way I was telling him. He would worry and I was afraid it would affect the way he played."

As if nothing was wrong, she and Bill traveled the 40 minutes to Lewisburg that night for Giles County's 29-8 win over Marshall County. With a playoff berth assured, O'Conner didn't ask Bo to do much more than hand off to Houston, who ran for 169 yards on 32 carries. Bo completed two of three passes for 83 yards and rushed six times for 30.

Bill and Trina were there again the next week for a home game against Bolivar Central to open the playoffs. Bo threw for only 63 yards, and the Bobcats managed just 199 yards total offense. Bolivar Central, 7-3 after the win, would lose two weeks later in the quarterfinal round to Lipscomb.

In his first full season as a starter, Bo led Giles County to an 8-3 record and his stats were solid: 100 of 170 passing (59 percent), 1,696 yards, 15 touchdowns, nine interceptions.

Trina took the playoff loss harder than most. "I remember asking Bill, 'What if that's the last game I ever see him play?' Bill told me, 'Don't talk like that. You're going to be fine.' But I wasn't sure.

"The only thing I was certain of was that I had to fight this because I wanted my kids to always fight and never give up. If they could see how hard I fought this horrible disease, maybe that would inspire them to fight for everything they want."

• • •

The day after the season-ending loss, Trina and Bill asked Bo and Baylee to sit down on the couch. Bo was 15, Baylee 12.

"We let Bryce go over to my mother's house," Trina said. "He was only six, so there was no way for him to understand.

"It was hard telling them. The first thing out of Bo's mouth was, 'Are you going to be OK?' I told him yes. Baylee wanted to know if I was going to lose my hair — leave it to a girl, right?" Trina laughed. "Bo got mad at her for asking that but it was a good question. I didn't want to lose my hair, either. I was almost as devastated about that as I was the diagnosis."

Bo asked question after question. "He wanted to know when I was going to find out about my treatments, so he went with Bill and me to my next appointment. He was bound and determined to hear everything Dr. Gian had to say.

"Bo is a quiet kid, so we never discussed my illness after that. But I knew he thought about it a lot. That's the way he handles things like this."

• • •

I had interviewed Bo dozens of times for this book before I finally asked him on the phone one night about his mom's bout with cancer.

I had rarely seen or heard him get emotional, but his voice cracked several times as he talked.

"She was unbelievable," he said. "Tough and strong. She didn't want us worried, so she just pretended everything was OK.

"She would go to treatment, go to work, come home, fix supper, and then go throw up because of the chemo. I've never seen anything like it. She's way tougher than me.

"My dad helped out a lot. He cooked some, too. But it was a scary thought that we could lose our mom — *bam!* — just like that. I don't think you ever get over that feeling. It just makes you appreciate her even more."

Billy Watkins 45

Bo managed to laugh.

"I remember when I was playing at Scooba, we would be in the huddle and the one voice I could hear from the stands was my mom's — *'Come on, Bo!* She would yell it real slow and real loud, and my teammates in the huddle would hear it, too. They would be like, 'Bo's mom is gettin' mad at us, let's go.'"

• • •

The chemo claimed Trina's hair.

She and Bill were at a Titans' game, and she was wearing a hoodie. "I had the hood up, and when I pulled it down a big clump of hair was in it," she said. "I think that hits every woman hard when they go through it. And I dreaded showing Baylee."

She finished her treatments in May 2008. About a month before Bo's junior season was set to begin, she underwent another CAT scan to see if any cancer cells were lingering.

The scan was clean, and she has remained cancer free.

"It's always in the back of my mind. *Always!* What if it comes back? What if the treatments have side effects that we don't know about that might show up later? All I know is, if it comes back I'll fight it just like I did the first time. My kids will always know I did everything in my power to take care of them and be there for them always."

Chapter 8

O'Conner expected Bo's passing numbers to dip his junior season. "We only had one really good receiver returning — and he tore his ACL the first game and was gone for the year. We knew we were going to have to run the ball, so we put just about everything on Bo and [senior running back] Tobias Houston."

Bo showed a well-rounded game as Giles County won six of its first seven games, losing only to Columbia Central, 42-28, in Week 5. Through those six games, Bo completed 59 of 93 (63 percent) passes for 735 yards, eight touchdowns, two interceptions; he rushed 57 times for 515 yards and eight touchdowns.

The Bobcats traveled to Nashville in Week 8 for another battle with Lipscomb, 7-0. O'Conner and offensive coordinator Thomas O'Steen decided running the football, primarily with Bo and Houston, provided the best shot at winning. They could chew up yards and, hopefully, drain the clock.

"We knew that the tougher the game and the tougher the situation, the better those guys ran the football," O'Conner said.

"And Coach O'Conner had really studied how to stop the Wing-T offense, which is what Lipscomb ran every year," Bill Wallace said. "He knew if we were ever going to win a state championship, we were going to have to be able to beat them."

As expected, the game was close throughout. Giles County broke the

14-14 halftime score with a 5-yard run by Houston with 1:06 left in the third quarter. Lipscomb scored twice early in the fourth quarter to go ahead, 28-21. Giles County answered late.

"Bo led us on a great drive there at the end," O'Conner said.

Bo's 1-yard sneak for a touchdown and the point-after kick tied the game, 28-28, with 2:34 remaining.

But Lipscomb dished out heartache again, winning 31-28 on a last-play, 27-yard field goal. Giles County had a hard time corralling Zach Rogers, a 6-foot-2, 170-pound speedster rated the No. 9 prospect in the state by Rivals and a future Tennessee Volunteer. Rogers gashed the Bobcats for touchdown runs of 68, 21, and 14 yards. He gained 163 yards on just six carries. He caught a 20-yard touchdown pass to open the scoring.

Bo rushed 28 times for 190 yards and one touchdown. He completed 5 of 8 passes for 50 yards and was intercepted once. Houston rushed 22 times for 92 yards and three touchdowns.

Giles County won its final two regular season games — at Creek Wood and at home against Marshall County. Two home victories to open the playoffs, 46-26 against McNairy Central and 13-6 over Page, set up a rematch with Lipscomb, 12-0. Once again, the Bobcats would have to travel to Nashville.

This one, too, featured last-second drama.

Bo's 8-yard touchdown run late in the third quarter put Giles County ahead, 10-3. Lipscomb made it 10-10 with 8:06 left in the fourth quarter.

As he took the field to try and lead his team to one of the biggest victories in school history, Bo remembers looking at the crowd. The stands were full and fans stood at the fence surrounding the field.

On the Lipscomb side were the city folks, who paid thousands of dollars a year to send their children to the private school. And many of the players were openly recruited to Lipscomb. On the other side were the blue-collar, hard-working folks of Giles County where, on average, only 9 percent — about half the national number — of the 29,000 residents earn a degree from a four-year college or university. Bo wouldn't have swapped sides if he could have, and he was determined to end his school's four-game losing streak to the Mustangs.

"Coach O'Conner used to say, 'Yeah, those Lipscomb guys have money and big houses. And they probably think they're a little bit better than y'all are,'" Bo recalls. "We didn't like hearing that a whole lot."

A methodical drive deep into Lipscomb territory came down to a fourth and eight with a little more than three minutes remaining. Bo dropped back to throw, couldn't find an open receiver, and scrambled to his right. He saw an open alley down the sideline and took off. A Lipscomb defender had an angle on Bo as he neared the spot needed for a first down.

Bo went airborne.

In photos, he appears to be flying, his body stretched parallel to the ground, his head and shoulders tilted back. People in Giles County refer to it as "The Superman" play, when he soared higher than the heads of people standing nearby.

First down, Giles County.

Houston put the Bobcats ahead 16-10 with a 12-yard run with 1:21 remaining. But they missed the point-after kick, a fundamental error that often proves heartbreaking in games fought this hard.

And so it was. The Mustangs scored on a 22-yard touchdown pass with 28 seconds left to tie the score, and they made their point-after kick to take the lead, 17-16. That is how it ended.

Bo passed for 74 yards, completing 6 of 11. He also rushed 19 times for 74 yards and a touchdown. Houston ran 20 times for 95 yards. Bo also made six tackles, second most on the team, and nabbed a crucial interception in the end zone just before halftime.

As a junior, Bo finished 99 of 164 passing (60 percent) for 1,243 yards, 12 touchdowns and five interceptions. He rushed 153 times for 1,137 yards and 13 scores.

"I really believe that because he'd thrown for 1,600 yards-plus his sophomore season, then dropped to 1,243 his junior season, a lot of colleges backed off," O'Conner said. "They didn't realize that our best receiver was

5-foot-5 and ran a 4.9 40. If they had just bothered to watch Bo's film and how he played and the things he did for us ... man, there are some things about football and recruiting that you just can't explain."

• • •

Even though the Bobcats hadn't delivered a state championship during Bo's first two seasons as a starter, football had become a hot topic again throughout the county.

Giles County's football stadium deteriorated during years of fielding mediocre teams. A section of the home bleachers was condemned and roped off with police tape.

Eighteen victories the past two seasons proved cause for action. In a countywide vote, citizens approved a renovation that would make it one of the nicest stadiums in south central Tennessee — and just in time for Bo's final go-round in 2009.

Chapter 9

Football has a bushel basket of sayings. One is: "He looks like a senior." That was certainly the case when Bo began his high school season. He stood a little over 6-foot-4 and weighed about 190. It was clear that Bo and 6-foot, 192-pound running back Tobias Houston — who rushed for 1,485 yards and 25 touchdowns as a junior — would have to carry the offensive load.

But Bo hoped his "recruiting" was going to pay off. Before the 2008 season, Bo had talked one of his best friends and former youth league teammate, Zach Bailey, into coming back out for football the year before. Bailey wasn't big — 5-foot-7, 150 pounds — but he was fast and sure-handed. Even though he had caught just six passes for 51 yards as a junior, Bo believed he could stretch the field like no one had the previous two seasons.

Like most folks in Giles County, Bo had anticipated opening night for months. He wanted to help bring a state championship to the county where he had grown up, the county in which his parents had become sweethearts during high school. He also hoped to show college coaches — especially those from the SEC — he was worthy of a scholarship.

But on the morning of the season opener, Bo came down with a stomach virus. So did Houston.

Both started and played. "But they were throwing up most of the game," O'Conner said.

Bo passed for 178 yards and two touchdowns, including a 38-yard score to Bailey. He rushed 17 times for another 100 yards to go with Houston's 123 yards and a touchdown. But a missed point-after kick proved to be the difference as Cookeville won, 25-24.

The two-and-a-half hour bus ride home seemed like 20.

One week later, Giles County christened its newly polished stadium with a 34-7 beat down of Lawrence County. That was the start of a dominant streak in which the Bobcats outscored opponents 366 to 67 and ended the regular season 9-1.

Through 10 games, Bo was 133 of 192 passing for 2,223 yards, 26 touchdowns and five interceptions.

A first-round playoff win over Chester County, 45-20, set up a battle Bo and his teammates had hoped would materialize. If this was going to be a championship season, they felt Lipscomb should be one of the victims.

"It was one of our goals — yeah, win the state was the main one, but we wanted to beat Lipscomb, too."

The Mustangs had won six straight and entered the game 8-3.

On Wednesday before the Friday night game, the Bobcats' starting middle linebacker, senior B.J. Morris, sprained his ankle.

"This was one of those games where you put all your chips on the table," O'Conner said. "We talked to Bo about filling in at middle linebacker, and he was all for it. He would've been a great linebacker, but we simply couldn't risk putting him down in there week after week.

"Lipscomb runs a lot of misdirection plays, but Bo's instincts were so good we knew he could read the plays and find the football."

Playing at home, Giles County led 13-0 late in the second quarter on touchdown runs by Houston of one and 13 yards. The Bobcats took over on its 23-yard line with a little more than two minutes left in the half. Lipscomb's defensive coaches guessed that Bo would try to hit Bailey on a long ball and played their secondary deep.

They guessed wrong. Offensive coordinator Thomas O'Steen called a quarterback draw. Bo ran 77 yards for a touchdown. Even another missed point-after couldn't dull the joy of leading 19-0 at halftime. And Giles

County was physically dominating its nemesis.

Lipscomb finally scored with a little more than six minutes left on a 7-yard run. Fittingly, its point-after was no good.

Bo answered with a touchdown run of nine yards. Final score: Giles County 32, Lipscomb 6.

Few victories in any sport up to that point felt as good as this one, Bo said. Lipscomb had defeated the Bobcats six straight times by an average score of 30-12.

"We were really tired of hearing about it," Bo said. "We definitely wanted to be the ones to end the streak, and we had been so close the year before."

He completed 8 of 8 passes for 83 yards. "We could've thrown more and been successful, no doubt about it," O'Conner said.

Instead, the Bobcats outrushed Lipscomb 402 to 125. Bo carried 16 times for 237 yards and two scores. Houston added 122 yards and a pair of scores. And Bo proved salty on defense with five tackles in part-time duty.

Giles County was in the state quarterfinals, three victories from a state championship. O'Conner pleaded with his seniors to show the rest of the team how to handle success — relish eliminating Lipscomb but remember the ultimate goal.

Bill was telling Bo the same thing at home.

• • •

Chester County entered the quarterfinal 9-3 but had won eight of its last nine.

The first half was a struggle. Bo hit Bailey on a 45-yard touchdown pass and Houston ran in a two-point conversion. The Bobcats led 8-3 at intermission.

Any letdown after the historic victory over Lipscomb died at halftime. Bo connected with Bailey on a 61-yard touchdown pass and also ran for a 7-yard touchdown to make it 22-10 entering the fourth quarter. Houston added touchdown runs of five and six yards. Giles County won, 36-10.

The semifinal was a matchup of similar teams. Like Giles County, the Liberty Tech Magnet Crusaders lost their first game but had won every week since. They had done so with a high-powered offense, scoring more than 40 points in nine of their victories.

Fighting to reach the championship game, the Bobcats' defense was stifling while the offense built a 21-7 lead through three quarters. The game ended 28-14. Bo was 20 of 26 passing for 246 yards and two touchdowns and also rushed for 106 yards and two scores.

Shirey still talks about Bo's three-yard scoring run in the third quarter. "He ran over a linebacker at the goal line. Kept it on an option play and just leveled him," he said.

Senior defensive end Josh Brewer led the Bobcats with 13 tackles. Linebacker B.J. Morris added 10.

And here is one of the beautiful things about high school football: Two defensive backs, senior Raheem Holt and junior Kanden Kimbrough — 5-foot-3, 125 pounds and 5-foot-4, 130 pounds, respectively — played much bigger than the program said. Each contributed 10 tackles against Liberty Tech. They were among the team's leading tacklers through four playoff games — Holt with 34, Kimbrough with 33. Kimbrough also had two interceptions.

O'Conner liked the grit of his team, top to bottom. And the Bobcats would need it in the championship game against Greeneville, 11-4 but a winner of nine straight.

• • •

Giles County was designated the visitor at Tennessee Tech University in Cookeville. The Bobcats took the field in the late-afternoon matchup wearing white jerseys with black numerals, gold pants and black helmets. Greeneville was just that — green head to toe except for white numerals and a white shoulder stripe.

It was a slugfest.

After a scoreless first quarter, Bo threw an 80-yard touchdown pass to Bailey. Greeneville tied it on a 17-yard run. It remained 7-7 through three quarters.

Early in the final period, Greeneville quarterback Wes Quarles ran an option keep 36 yards to put the Green Devils ahead 14-7.

Giles County answered, with Bo driving the Bobcats for the tying score — a 4-yard touchdown pass to Josh Smith — with 7:14 left.

With under four minutes left, Greeneville fumbled a punt and Giles County's Fred Appleton recovered at the Bobcats' 30. Two plays netted just two yards. On third-and-8 and time running short, Giles County enjoyed the fruits of its game plan.

"We had run short and intermediate pass routes most of the night, just wanting to keep the ball away from Greeneville," O'Conner said. "And we'd done a good job of it and maybe set them up for a big play."

On third and 8, Bo dropped back and let loose a high, tight spiral down the left sideline. The ball traveled 55 yards to Zach Bailey, who caught it in stride at the 16 and raced into the end zone for the go-ahead touchdown. Mitch Byrd's third point-after kick made it 21-14.

Greeneville desperately drove inside Giles County territory. In the final seconds, Quarles' pass over the middle and near the goal line was intercepted by Kimbrough — his second of the game.

Giles County had won its first state championship in school history, and Bo's performance was legendary.

The *Knoxville News-Sentinel* reported it this way:

"Giles County quarterback Bo Wallace lived up to his Mr. Football billing Saturday night.

Big arm. Mobility. Leader."

Greeneville coach Caine Ballard called Bo "a great quarterback on a good football team."

He finished 18 of 29 for 315 yards, 2 touchdowns, no interceptions.

While Greeneville held Houston to 27 yards on nine carries, Bo rushed 15 times for 64 yards.

Bo put up astounding numbers as a senior: 205 of 293 passing (70 percent) for 3,288 yards, 37 touchdowns and five interceptions. Yet he left the field that night with one school willing to offer him a scholarship — UT-Martin.

"It's still a mystery to me why no major schools were interested," O'Conner said.

. . .

A little more than a month after the state championship game, a major football power was interested: LSU.

Bo, along with his parents and O'Conner, visited Baton Rouge. While standing on the field at Tiger Stadium during a tour of the team's facilities, a man walked up wearing a tattered fishing hat and some knock-around clothes. He greeted them, and then said: "Let's go up and talk."

Bill Wallace let the others walk ahead and motioned for O'Conner to hold up.

"Who is this cat?" Bill whispered.

O'Conner thought he was kidding.

"Man, that's Les Miles."

"Les Miles? I thought the guy was the groundskeeper."

They still laugh about that moment.

Miles had just completed his fifth season as head coach of the Tigers and was only three years removed from winning the Bowl Championship Series national championship. He won 34 games his first three seasons in Baton Rouge, but the Tigers had slipped to 8-5 in 2008 and 9-4 in 2009. Jordan Jefferson had started 12 games during the '09 season as a sophomore but was inconsistent. Behind him on the depth chart was Jarrett Lee, who started eight games as a redshirt freshman and was remembered best for throwing seven interceptions that were returned for touchdowns in 2008.

He played sparingly in '09,

Bo believed he could compete for playing time running offensive coordinator Gray Crowton's pro-style offense.

Miles was straight up with Bo, his family, and O'Conner.

"Bo is the No. 2 quarterback on our board, and we're only taking one quarterback in this recruiting class," Miles said. "We think the guy ahead of him is going to commit this coming week. But if another SEC school calls and is interested in Bo, call me right then."

True to his word, Miles only signed one quarterback in that recruiting class, the prospect he told them about — Zach Lee, a 6-foot-4, 200-pounder from McKinney, Texas. And Lee did, indeed, commit the next week.

But Lee never played a down for LSU.

He went through summer workouts and two weeks of fall camp at LSU before signing a $5.25 million baseball contract with the Los Angeles Dodgers' organization. A right-handed pitcher, Lee was the 28th player selected in the 2010 Major League draft.

The Dodgers named Lee their minor league Pitcher of the Year in 2013. Entering 2015, Lee had earned a spot on the Dodgers' 40-man roster and worked his way up to Triple A Oklahoma City.

Bo Wallace, his parents and his siblings

Chapter 10

April 11, 2014, Six Days After Spring Game

It started about the fourth or fifth practice of spring training.

"And every practice after that, it just grew and grew and grew," Bo said.

He was talking about the chemistry and confidence of the 2014 Ole Miss Rebels, and he had plenty to say.

"I've been part of championship teams, in high school and again in junior college," he said. "I've never experienced anything quite like this. We competed every single day. I'm talking about the older guys like me and Vince [Sanders] and D.T. [Shackelford] and Cody [Prewitt] and C.J. [Johnson]. And the young guys did, too. Quon [Treadwell]. Robert [Nkemdiche]. Tony [Conner]. Laremy [Tunsil].

"When you sign a class like we did in 2013 — full of stars and highly-recruited players — the one thing you wonder is 'How hard will they work?' For a lot of players like that, football has been easy. They've never been really challenged. They've never had to give 100 percent on every play. They've gotten by because of pure talent or because they were bigger and stronger than everybody else. But this 2013 bunch brings it. They did last year, right from the start, and they're doing it even more now.

"And I've got to give props to the coaches. They brought it every single day, too. The way a coach comes out and pushes his [position] group to work and get better. You can't have some groups giving it all they've got and a couple other groups just sort of out there. Our coaches were running all over the place, celebrating when players made plays, getting on them and coaching them when they messed up something. And if one side of the ball was a little more into it than the other, Coach Freeze would call them out. He'd be like, 'OK, offensive coaches, get your energy up over there. You're getting' *whipped!*' It made practice fun.

"Our team is just so together now. On our previous two teams, we had some good guys who competed and played hard. But I can't say we were united as one. You had the offense, and you had the defense. That's changed. We are all so close. It's hard to describe it, but you can definitely feel it. When you hear Coach Freeze saying more and more players are buying in to the program and the way he wants things done, that's because they are. And the more people bought in, the better we practiced. I think at some point everybody just sort of looked around and said, 'Damn, we're good! This team can be special.' I think we are all looking forward to the season getting here and seeing what we can do."

Personally, Bo said "I got more out of this spring than any I've been through.

"They limited my reps. The coaches didn't want to overwork my shoulder, wanted it to come along slowly. It was spent by the time the bowl game was over. Plus, I know they wanted to look at the younger quarterbacks and see what they could do. But I felt great, physically and mentally.

"The game has slowed down so much. I remember my sophomore year and how fast everything was in that Texas game [a 66-31 loss in Oxford]. But now I'm seeing things happen before they ever develop. There isn't much a defense can throw at me that I haven't seen at one point or another."

Werner commented on that after the spring game.

"We're able to give Bo more responsibility after he comes to the line as far as changing plays," Werner said. "One time today on a third down and nine, the defense was going to bring a zone blitz, and the defensive end was going to drop right beneath the route that Laquon was running. Bo saw it, gave Quon another route and got the first down. That's a lot of growth and maturity on Bo's part."

Bo went to Werner the last week of spring drills and asked for more reps.

"I'd had a good spring but there was a point where I started feeling rusty. I didn't want to end the spring like that. Coach Werner and Coach Freeze understood and were real good about it. I got more reps the last few days."

Bo completed 10 of 21 passes in the spring game for 152 yards, one touchdown and no interceptions.

When discussing the spring's top surprises, Bo mentioned the same players as Freeze — wide receiver Collins Moore and cornerback Cliff Coleman. Moore earned the Eli Manning Award as Most Improved Offensive Player. Coleman received the Jeff Hamm Memorial Award for Most Improved Defensive Player.

Moore, a senior, had shown flashes of brilliance in practices but couldn't stay healthy. He sustained injuries to both shoulders in 2013.

"He caught everything this spring. He could really help us," Bo said.

Bo called Coleman "a lockdown corner who played a lot more physical this spring, which really helps our depth over there."

On May 17, Bo planned to travel to Los Angeles for five days to workout under football's newest quarterback guru — former Major League pitcher and coach Tom House.

House runs the Rod Dedeaux Research and Baseball Institute. He was previously known for serving as pitching coach of Nolan Ryan while with the Texas Rangers — and also for catching Hank Aaron's 715th home run, which broke Babe Ruth's career record. A left-handed relief pitcher, House was in the Atlanta Braves' bullpen at old Atlanta-Fulton County Stadium on April 8, 1974, the night The Hammer passed The Babe.

I was familiar with House's beliefs that the throwing motion of pitchers and quarterbacks are closely related. While on a newspaper assignment in 1989, I arrived early at a Texas Rangers game in Arlington to interview former Mississippi State star Rafael Palmeiro. I saw the Rangers' pitching staff throwing footballs in the outfield before batting practice.

"Footballs? What's that all about?" I asked Palmeiro.

"Tom House, man. He thinks outside the box," he said.

In his Hall of Fame induction speech, Ryan referred to House as "a coach that is always on the cutting edge."

House pitched eight seasons in the big leagues with the Braves, Boston Red Sox, Toronto Blue Jays, and Seattle Mariners. He retired following the 1978 season with a 29-23 record, 33 saves and a 3.79 earned run average. Since going into private business, House had mainly worked with pitchers until NFL quarterback Drew Brees sought his advice following a serious shoulder injury in the final game of the 2005 regular season. Brees credits House with helping save his career, which includes a Super Bowl title with the New Orleans Saints four years after the injury.

Since then, quarterbacks have sought House's tips and secrets, including the New England Patriots' Tom Brady, the Baltimore Ravens' Joe Flacco, and the Kansas City Chiefs' Alex Smith.

"Coach Werner saw a segment about him on HBO's *Real Sports*," Bo said. "He and our trainer, Pat Jernigan, called out there. My family has to pay for my workouts, but I really want to go out and let [House] look at my shoulder, my throwing motion, my footwork and help get me back to the way I was before the injury. Then I'll come back and rep everything he tells me to do for the rest of the summer and into the season. It's an eight-week program, and I won't miss a day. I want to do anything and everything I can to help this team. We can tell we are close to doing something special."

Chapter 11

June 6, 2014, Oxford

Bo was different from the last time I visited with him.

He was now a college graduate, earning his degree in May in general studies with minors in history and education.

He also was a different quarterback than he'd been the past two seasons. His passes had more zip, and he was making throws he couldn't the past two years because of the shoulder injury and subsequent surgery.

"It was visible as soon as we started our summer workouts," Senquez Golson told me following a game in October. "I'd never seen Bo with that much speed on the ball. I never mentioned it to him. I'd just tell him, 'Good job today.' I didn't want to mess with his mind or anything. He seemed to be in a good place. But I could definitely tell his shoulder was healthy again. and I realized just how much the injury had hindered him before."

Bo even managed to smile after throwing an interception during a summer workout.

"Trae Elston picked me," he said, "and he came running over, shaking his hands and saying 'Man, your arm is back! That hurt to catch it.'

"I knew I was throwing it better. I know my body. I know how the ball is supposed to feel coming out of my hand. Everybody talks about how easy I made it look at Scooba, and how the ball just flew out of my hand.

Well, my arm is going to be stronger than it was at Scooba."

• • •

The five days working under Tom House in Los Angeles were more helpful than he had imagined.

"I feel like I know so much more now about myself ... fundamental things to keep my motion in check to make sure I'm doing things the right way," he said.

"The first thing they did was put these pod things all over my body and videotape my throwing motion using eight cameras in a circle. They could show my motion from all these different angles, my release point, any head movement I had when throwing, the torque I was able to get throwing the ball, my hand speed. Just about anything you can think of. Their thinking is, if you can see what you're doing, then you can correct it and go on the field and feel yourself doing it the right way."

One flaw House and his staff pointed out immediately was too much head movement.

"Tom House was really into that because head movement destroys a pitcher's accuracy," Bo said. "They said with a quarterback one inch of head movement creates six inches of inaccuracy. So the past two seasons, if I was throwing an out from the opposite hash, I'd really have to try and muscle it out there because of the shoulder. My head was all over the place. I can't even begin to imagine how much accuracy that cost me.

"Then we started doing different drills. They put a towel under our non-throwing arm. That keeps your shoulder tucked and keeps you from spinning out of a throw. We talked about opposite and equal, meaning ever how high my throwing hand is, my front hand is supposed to be at the same height.

"I threw a lot of weighted balls — 2 pounds, 1 pound, half a pound. I'd probably throw 50 or 60 balls a day. Just enough to build fundamentals and show me what I need to be doing every day."

House, who has a doctorate in psychology, also put Bo through a written psychological test.

"It was really cool," Bo said. "One thing they suggested I do is every night before I brush my teeth, I'm supposed to write down three things I will make sure I get done the next day. It will keep me from procrastinating."

And what did he have written down for today?

"Hmm, let's see. I wrote down that I would go through every drill I was supposed to. I'd do all the stretches they taught me. And I'd do my footwork drills after our seven-on-seven voluntary workout."

And?

"Yep, I've done all three."

. . .

Bo asked Trina to email me a copy of his psychological test. It's called The Flippen Profile: An Introduction to Personal Growth & Personal Constraint Theory. The test is designed to "help you identify the key Personal Constraints that may be limiting your effectiveness personally and professionally."

Bo scored "on target" in seven categories: Self Critical, Adaptive Child, Self Confidence, Need for Achievement, Dominance, Need to Engage In Nurturing Behavior. and Need for Affiliation.

He scored above the target in four areas: Aggressiveness/Competitiveness, Need for Change and Variety, Desire for Encouragement and Emotional Support, Critical Thought Process.

In the end, the test confirmed what most of his coaches, teammates, friends, family, and fans already knew: Bo is self confident, feels a need to lead, can make impulsive decisions, expects a lot of those around him, possesses a stronger will to win than most, able to perform in stressful situations, doesn't mind speaking his mind, and isn't afraid of challenges.

Take any of those traits away — even the impulsive decisions — and you don't have the quarterback who took Ole Miss to two straight bowls his sophomore and junior seasons.

• • •

"I hate to bring it up," I said, "but that's awful about Chief."

Chief Brown suffered a torn Achilles during conditioning workouts just a couple of days earlier. He is expected to miss the 2014 season, and his absence hurts the depth in the secondary. Chief played significant snaps at free safety and rover in 2013 and was behind Tony Conner on the depth chart at Husky headed into fall camp.

"Man, he is taking it hard, and I'm sick about it," Bo said. "He is such a good guy. Now, don't get me wrong, he's still a nerd. Anybody who will fuss at you for paying 15 cents more than he thinks you should for a pack of cheese is a nerd."

Bo laughed and shook his head.

"Chief and Denzel were the first two guys who tried to be my friend when I got to Ole Miss. That's how we wound up rooming together. Chief didn't like me at first because me and Denzel were becoming buddies. Chief looked at it like I was stealing his friend. But we all three became really close.

"I'm just telling him to keep his head up and work hard to rehab it, and you never know. He might get back and play some this season. I hope so. I don't want to play my last season here without him."

Chapter 12

July 23, 2014, Oxford

We agreed to meet at a restaurant on The Square before he headed home to Pulaski for a few days. Fall camp was set to begin a week later.

I arrived a few minutes early and walked toward an empty table ... then I stopped and turned around. I had just walked past Bo and didn't recognize him. He smiled as I threw up my hands and said, "I'm sorry, but I was looking for Bo Wallace."

He was wearing a baseball cap backward, a white V-neck t-shirt and blue Ole Miss gym shorts. He was bigger than I'd ever seen him. He looked like a linebacker.

"Dude, you are huge," I said as we shook hands.

"Yeah, I'm hearing that a lot," he said. "I've even had people ask me if I'm doing steroids. I tell them, 'No, I'm not taking steroids. I've been able to lift weights for the first time during an entire off-season.'

"I weigh 228. I'll lose some during two-a-days, and then during the wear and tear of the season. But this will help me stay healthy, help me be stronger in the pocket and running the ball. I feel good. It's been a great summer."

For the most part, he meant.

His prediction came true earlier this month at the SEC Media Days in Birmingham, where all 14 head coaches and a couple of star players from each team are interviewed by sportswriters and broadcasters from across the South: The media voted Auburn's Nick Marshall the first-team All-SEC quarterback, and Mississippi State's Dak Prescott second team.

"That's total bullshit," he said. "Marshall deserves it. The dude has paid his dues and won a bunch of games, took Auburn to the national championship game. But Dak Prescott ... if we play anywhere near our potential last November, we aren't even having this conversation. But because they beat us in overtime and he came off the bench in the fourth quarter, and then put up a bunch of numbers against Rice in the freakin' Liberty Bowl, now he's one of the two best quarterbacks in the league.

"He may be good. But to me, he hasn't shown it over enough games to be voted second team All-SEC. He's a nice enough guy. I was around him some at the Manning camp. We'd speak, like 'What's up?' But we didn't do a lot of chatting. It's nothing personal toward him. It's just one quarterback against another. I'm just glad we get to play each other one more time, and we'll see how that works out."

He learned of the media's vote from Kyle Campbell during the trip to Birmingham.

"I wasn't surprised," he said "I told you back in January it was going to happen. But that's OK. This whole 'Dak Knight Rises' crap that State has cooked up has done nothing but motivate me.

"I've almost become obsessed with being the best. During the spring and summer, I thought about it every night. I'd be in bed thinking about how much I want to help this team win, and I'd jump out of bed and do 20 or 30 pushups, get some water and go back to bed. I know that sounds crazy but that's how bad I want us to have a great season."

I asked him if anyone had surprised him during summer workouts.

"Dayall Harris," he said, referring to the true freshman wide receiver from Callaway High School in Jackson. "The guy is a freak athlete. He could wind up playing a lot this year. He catches everything, and he goes up and makes unbelievable plays."

Bo had several individual school records within his grasp. He trailed Eli

Manning in career total offense by 2,899, in career passing yards by 3,779, in number of wins as a starting quarterback by nine.

"I see those numbers all the time," he said. "There's a huge picture of Eli on the wall leading into the dressing room with his career numbers, so it's not like it's not in my face every day. I'd love to get some of the records, but to be honest I'm not sure the fans want me to break them. I understand how they feel about the Mannings, and I don't blame them."

I assured him if it meant winning the SEC West Division, the fans would applaud him passing Eli in every category imaginable.

"Yeah, I guess," he said with a shrug. "But the record I'd like the most is to be the first quarterback to lead Ole Miss to the SEC championship game, and win it. That is the biggest thing to me. That's my job, do my part to get us there."

"Has the fact that your senior season is right here in front of you hit you yet?" I asked. "Are you already going 'This will be my last summer workout' and 'this will be my last fall camp'?"

"I am," he said, nodding. "It's gone by so fast. I want to try and take everything in, soak it all up. Enjoy the journey. And work and prepare like never before. I'm not saying I didn't prepare hard my first two years, but I know there were things I could have done better. Maybe not go out as much. Watch a little more film. But I think every senior looks back and says that.

"But it's time for me to be a gym rat. Stay in the Manning Center and mean business while I'm there."

I asked about his shoulder.

"It's fine. It's structurally sound, and I'm throwing better than I have since I first hurt it my sophomore year. I can't wait to get started. I remember how frustrating the 2013 camp was. I'd had surgery and I guess the guys thought I was going to be like my old self as soon as I walked out there the first practice. But I couldn't start throwing until June, and then it was 20 throws from five yards away into a net.

"I think the receivers and even some of the coaches got frustrated when I couldn't put the ball exactly where it needed to be during my first few practices. I kept saying, 'I'm going to get it right, just be a little patient.' Look, I had my doubts, too. My shoulder was so bad. I couldn't drive with my right arm. I couldn't raise it up high enough to put my hand on the steering wheel. I had some doubt. I was like, 'Will I be the same quarterback I was before?' But it slowly came around, and by the end of fall camp I was throwing the ball pretty good.

"I'm just happy I don't have to deal with that this fall camp. I can go out there and let it rip. I'm sure the coaches will monitor me and not let me overdo it. But I'm ready to go."

I asked him if there is one game that he has circled on the schedule.

"Yep. Tennessee," he said. "I don't have to tell you State and Alabama are circled. But Tennessee is one I'm really glad is on our schedule. I've wanted to play them since they wouldn't give me the time of day out of high school, and I can't wait to get them here, though I almost wish we were playing them in Knoxville. My teammates know how much that game means to me, too."

I asked, "What are your true expectations for this team? I know you feel like y'all can beat anybody on the schedule, but what's a realistic goal?"

"I'm being realistic when I tell you we can win the West if we can stay healthy and get some breaks. Every team that wins it gets some breaks along the way," he said. "But I will tell you this today, sitting right here. We're going to beat Alabama. And we're going to beat State. Those two you can go ahead and mark down. People may think I'm out of my mind by saying that, but I know our coaches, I know our team and I know what we're capable of doing. Wait and see. October 4th. We will beat Alabama."

I posed the question everybody wanted to ask: Is he going to make a devoted effort to cut down on interceptions this season?

"Passing-wise, I would like to complete between 68 and 70 percent of my passes and throw no more than seven interceptions. I don't want to throw any, but if I can keep it down to about seven I'll be happy. Touchdown passes will come if my completion percentage is up where I want it to be. And if I'm throwing touchdown passes, that means we're scoring and winning ball games.

"It's not lost on me that how I play directly affects the outcome. Nobody has to tell me that. I know it and I live with it every day. But I don't dwell on it. If you thought all the time about how many people's happiness is in your hands every Saturday, it would drive you nuts. So I just don't let my mind go there."

I asked: "When you throw that first pick — and every quarterback is going to throw them — have you thought about how you'll react? Will you be so angry you'll have to calm yourself down? Will you just shrug it off as part of the game? How will you handle it?"

A smile slowly crossed his face.

"I threw 17 my sophomore year," he said. "I've had a lot of practice handling them. I'll be OK."

Chapter 13

Bo sounded stressed two nights before the August 28 season opener against Boise State in the Chik-fil-a Kickoff Game in Atlanta's Georgia Dome.

"I don't think they match up with us athletically at all," he said. "But it's just hard trying to get a grip on what their plan will be on defense, and I think maybe that's why I'm more nervous than usual before an opener. They have just about everybody back on defense. Plus, we have a lot of new guys on the offensive line. Boise State plays really hard. That's sort of been their identity for years. We'll just have to take it series by series and adjust if we need to."

The reason for all the uncertainty was the Broncos' new coach, Bryan Harsin. He played quarterback at Boise State (1995-99) and was an assistant for 10 seasons (2001-2010), the final five as offensive coordinator. Harsin was co-offensive coordinator of the 2012 Texas team that hung 66 points on Freeze's first Rebel squad. Harsin followed Freeze and Auburn's Gus Malzahn as head coach at Arkansas State in 2013, when the Red Wolves were 7-5.

He replaced Chris Petersen, who was 92-12 in eight seasons while turning the blue-turf Broncos into giant slayers. Under Petersen, they defeated teams such as Oklahoma, Virginia Tech. and Oregon. They beat Georgia, 35-21, in the 2011 Chik-fil-a Kickoff Game.

But Petersen took the job at the University of Washington following the 2013 season when the Broncos were 8-5 — equaling the number of losses they had suffered in the previous five seasons combined. So the question remains: Was 2013 an exception or the beginning of a downward spiral?

A deeper reason for Bo and the offense to be concerned was Harsin's choice as defensive coordinator: Marcel Yates, who was co-defensive coordinator at Texas A&M the previous two seasons. The good news was Ole Miss scored 65 points in the two games combined. The bad news was the Rebels lost two heartbreakers to the Aggies in Oxford, and Yates learned plenty about the Rebels' scheme and personnel. Prior to that he was a defensive assistant at Boise State from 2003-2011.

"This is the hardest game to prepare for I can remember," Freeze said at his Monday press conference. "New head coach. New coordinators. No common opponents. It has been rather difficult. Boise is a really good team. They're a solid team and it's going to be a great challenge. We've tried to prepare for everything.

"We've studied quite a bit of every staff he's been on," said Freeze. "You can bet they'll be sound at what they do. It's not as comfortable as you'd like for it to be. He's been an offensive guy, so you'd think it would have his flavor to it."

Bo said one way the Rebels planned to counter any "surprise" defense by Boise State was to go up-tempo. "That way, we don't have to worry so much about what they do because they're having to adjust to us on the fly."

Fall camp "went really fast up until the last few days," he said. "Now, time is dragging. I wish we could play the dang game right now."

The offensive line remained the largest question mark, but there was a good starting point: Sophomore Laremy Tunsil was as great a player as there was at left tackle in college football. He stood 6-foot-5, 315 pounds and moved like a linebacker. He allowed one sack as a freshman.

Rated the No. 1 offensive tackle in the nation out of Lake City, Florida by most recruiting sites, he reportedly was considering only two schools in mid-January — Alabama and Georgia.

"None of the players had ever heard of Laremy until he showed up for his visit," Bo said. "I know I hadn't. I was like, 'Who is *that* guy?' I mean, he looked like an NFL lineman. Word started getting around that he was the best left tackle prospect in the country and that we were going to get him. That's the sort of thing a quarterback loves hearing."

But past Tunsil, the offensive line would be a work in progress.

It took a huge hit when the No. 3 tackle prospect in 2013 — 6-foot-5, 309-pound sophomore Austin Golson — transferred to Auburn after having a standout spring with Ole Miss. He was expected to start at right tackle. He started 12 games at right guard as a true freshman after de-committing from Florida State and signing with Ole Miss. Golson also had offers from Alabama, Auburn, Southern Cal, Stanford, and several more schools. He informed Freeze after spring drills that he wanted to move closer to his ailing grandparents in Alabama. Surprisingly, Freeze agreed to release him to attend any school, including an SEC West opponent. NCAA rules forced Golson to sit out the 2014 season.

Junior left guard Aaron Morris was talented and experienced but he was coming off a torn ACL that cost him most of the 2013 season. Right guard Justin Bell started all 13 games in 2013 but entered camp listed at 352 pounds; many wondered if he could hold up at that weight. Junior college transfer Fahn Cooper — yes, one of the two linemen Bo showed around Oxford the week after the Egg Bowl loss and was criticized for being out on the town — had earned the start at right tackle.

The center position remained unsettled. Junior Ben Still was named the starter, but inexperienced junior Robert Conyers also figured to play against the Broncos.

"It is what it is right now," Bo said of the offensive line. "They'll get better as the season goes on, and I know they'll play hard. Justin Bell has stepped up and been the vocal leader of the bunch. But I know I'm gonna have to get the ball out of my hand. I can't stand back there forever."

Who did he prefer at center between Still and Conyers? It was an important issue because 99.9 percent of Ole Miss' plays are run out of a shotgun formation.

"Makes no difference to me," he said. "Robert snaps the ball a little harder, but they're basically the same. They'll both scrap. That's what I care about. I want people up there who will play like it's their last play on earth. And I want linemen that if I get on their ass about something, they won't sulk. They play harder.

"I think this line will play hard for me. They know I care about them. I've made sure of that. I tell them when they do a good job. I tell them how important they are to the team. And I'm not just saying that stuff. I mean it."

. . .

Fall camp claimed two key defensive backs for the season: Junior college transfer Tee Shepard — who had four picks in one scrimmage — was sidelined after toe surgery. He was considered one of the best cornerback prospects to ever wear the Red and Blue. Junior Carlos Davis suffered a torn ACL, and that was a double whammy. He was expected to provide depth at corner and also return kicks.

But without question Ole Miss entered 2014 more talented and deeper overall — especially on defense — than it had been in years. It was ranked No. 18 in the Associated Press preseason poll — highest to open a season since 2009.

"Our defense is going to give people hell," Bo said. "I go against them, and I can tell you as a quarterback that it is no fun. Coach Wommack has them coming from every direction possible, and they are really physical, really fast. [Freshman] Marquis Haynes and C.J. [Johnson] have to be two of the fastest ends in the country. They're going to put a lot of pressure on quarterbacks. And we are really good in the secondary."

He was referring to senior All-American Cody Prewitt and junior Trae Elston at safety, senior Senquez Golson and junior Mike Hilton at the corners, and sophomore Tony Conner at Husky, which is basically a strong safety in Wommack's 4-2-5 scheme.

Before we hung up, I asked Bo if he was concerned about trying too hard to get the offense rolling in the early part of the game.

"I was actually thinking about that today," he said. "It's possible. But I'm going to have to talk myself down, calm myself, try and let the game develop, and make plays when they're there. But, yeah, that's something I am going to have to fight against."

Chapter 14

It was an ESPN prime time Thursday night game. The Rebels and Broncos had the world's TV football stage to themselves.

The broadcast team consisted of veterans Rece Davis, Todd Blackledge, and David Pollack.

Ole Miss was the designated home team and dressed accordingly: red jerseys, gray pants, navy blue headgear. Geography also made the Rebels the home team, with a majority of the 32,823 wearing Ole Miss red.

When Bo walked out of the tunnel along with his fellow team captains — Prewitt and long snapper Will Denny — he had no way of knowing he was about to play two quarters that would haunt him the rest of the season.

The nightmare started on the second possession when he threw an interception on first down from the Ole Miss 27. He was trying to connect with Evan Ingram on a seam route between the two safeties. Blackledge, a former Penn State quarterback and a longtime football analyst, said the pass "was a little late and allowed the backside safety to come over and make the play."

It continued on the first possession of the second quarter — another interception thrown on third and six at the Boise State 24.

And he was picked again, this time in the end zone, with 4 minutes, 45 seconds left in the half on third and 17 from the Boise State 20.

There was one highlight: His 30-yard touchdown pass to junior wideout Cody Core that put Ole Miss ahead, 7-0, with 57 seconds left in the first quarter.

The Rebels led 7-3 at halftime.

Freeze looked shell shocked as an ESPN sideline reporter asked him about Bo's first half performance.

"I think he's just trying too hard," he said. "He's made some really poor decisions that were really not even part of the progression. You know, we've just got to get in there and settle him down."

He called his team's seven false start penalties "embarrassing" and added "that's on me." He said he was proud of the defense and special teams. "But offensively, it hasn't been fun to watch."

Bo was 13 of 22 for 148 yards, one touchdown, and three interceptions. Boise State quarterback Grant Hedrick was having his own issues: 14 of 20 passing with three interceptions, by Golson, Johnson, and Prewitt.

Inside the Ole Miss dressing room, teammates were patting Bo on the shoulder pads and telling him to keep his head up.

Freeze had been correct in his assessment. "I was trying to do too much," Bo said. "I'd heard all off-season that my arm was weak, I'd been voted behind Marshall and Prescott at Media Days. All that was in my mind, and I was trying to prove them wrong instead of just letting the game come to me.

"It wasn't like every throw had been bad. We were moving the ball, but then I'd make that one throw that would get intercepted. I was confident things would change in the second half."

Social media was abuzz about Bo's three interceptions. So were the TV announcers.

"Bo Wallace comes back and has the most experience in the SEC," said Pollack, the former Georgia defensive end, "but he didn't look like it the first half. He's playing like a guy who doesn't know where he wants to go with the football."

Davis pointed out that Boise State outgained Ole Miss 203 to 168, and that Freeze's offense rushed for only 20 yards on 11 carries and converted on just 1 of 7 third downs. Boise State had rushed 22 times for 89 yards and thrown for 114.

Blackledge said of Ole Miss: "They've got to find a way to run the football in this second half. They're too one-dimensional, and their quarterback is not having a hot hand of a game ... Even though they're trailing, Boise State has shown much better balance."

Ole Miss got the ball to open the third quarter, and Bo was 3 of 3 for 46 yards as he guided the Rebels from their 25 to the Boise State 18. But Freeze inserted backup DeVante Kincade as a "wildcat" quarterback, and a poor snap coupled with a stout Boise State defensive front forced a loss of two.

The play before that, Bo kept on third-and-1 and was hit head-on by Boise State linebacker Ben Weaver. Wallace repeatedly assured the medical staff, "I'm OK, I'm good."

He wasn't. "I was actually knocked out for a second. And I felt something in my left shoulder."

He went back in on Ole Miss' next possession, which netted just one first down. Boise State then moved from its 32 to the Ole Miss 26. Dan Goodale kicked a 43-yard field goal to make it 7-6 with 1:02 left in the third quarter.

Though they hadn't relinquished the lead, the Rebels knew Boise State was gaining momentum entering the final period.

"I remember thinking 'This can be good for us,'" Bo said. "We knew we were better than they were, but it seemed like everything had gone against us. The interceptions, the penalties, getting stopped on fourth down inside their 20. It was the fourth quarter, and that's what we had trained for all offseason — be strong in the fourth quarter."

Strong, they were.

On their four fourth-quarter possessions — not counting two kneel down plays to end the game — the Rebels put together touchdown drives of 75, 76, 73, and 40 yards.

Bo threw three touchdown passes — 14 yards to Treadwell, 31 yards to Quincy Adeboyejo and 76 to Core. Ole Miss had pulled away 28-6 with 7:45

left in the game. The TD passes came during a stretch of 4 minutes, 41 seconds.

The TV announcers raved about Bo's turnaround.

Said Pollack: "To his credit, he's a guy who has taken a lot of flak over the years. You could tell by talking to him yesterday ... the coaches believe in him, and he believes in himself. To come out and throw three picks and be playing that poorly and rebound as well as he has, it says something about that young man."

Blackledge quickly added: "It does. But I still think for him to go to the next level, and to take Ole Miss to the next level — which is what they all want to do — he's got to clean that up. That touchdown to interception ratio as a senior, you need to be a plus 15, maybe a plus 20 ratio. And he knows that. He got away with it tonight, but you're not going to get away with it in SEC competition."

After Boise State scored on a 9-yard pass, the Rebels' Mark Dodson answered with a 19-yard touchdown run with 1:35 left.

Final score: Ole Miss 35, Boise State 13.

After the miserable start, Bo completed 18 of 21 for 239 yards, three touchdowns and no interceptions in the second half. In the fourth quarter, he was 6 of 7 for 175 yards.

For the game, Bo finished 25 of 36 for 387 yards, 4 touchdowns, 3 interceptions. And he did so without a quarterback's best friend — a running game. Ole Miss put up 458 yards of offense but only rushed for 71 yards on 34 carries.

Boise State managed 399 yards total offense, but Wommack's defensive unit only gave up 46 yards rushing the second half, and Tony Conner grabbed Ole Miss' fourth interception.

But the numbers don't speak to the defense's physical nature. Time and again, it delivered vicious blows in open space. At one point in the second half, Boise State's receivers were noticeably timid while running routes across the middle of the field.

It was a performance befitting a unit that had become known as "the

Landsharks" — circling and attacking when they smelled blood. It began in 2008 when former Iraqi war veteran Tony Fein, a linebacker, flashed a shark fin sign on the front of his helmet during the 2008 victory at LSU. Fein died in 2009 but his legacy grows with each "fins up" salute. The players and fans grew to love it. Coaches started using it as a recruiting tool.

"We're the one and only Landshark defense in the nation," Prewitt said post-game. "We have expectations to live up to every week."

Shackelford, Haynes, and John Youngblood had sacks, and the defense made 10 tackles for loss.

And a new weapon stepped forward in the first American football game he ever played in.

A 21-year-old redshirt freshman, Will Gleeson of Melbourne, Australia, punted four times for a net average of 47.8 yards. Three of his punts pinned Boise State inside its 10-yard line.

"I was real nervous," Gleeson said. "I'd never punted in a game with those big guys from another team running straight at me. I feel better having played a game now and understanding the 'feel' of it."

His performance would earn him the National Punter of the Week Award from the College Football Performance Awards, and the Ray Guy Award Player of the Week by the Augusta, Georgia Sports Council.

• • •

At his postgame press conference, Freeze addressed Bo's performance: "How many times has the question been asked about 'how is Bo Wallace and what do you expect of him?' He wants to do so well and have such a great year ... we were always behind the chains, and I'm sure he felt that we've got to press a little bit. So, he obviously didn't play his best. I thought he settled in the second half and played pretty good."

• • •

Bo met the press in a hallway outside the dressing room. He sat in a metal chair. He wore a red baseball cap turned backward.

What was the difference in the two halves?

"Just settling down, playing football, and not trying to make too much happen, things like that," he said.

A reporter asked: "Coach Werner said on one of the interceptions, the defensive back just made a good play. On the other two what did you see? What went wrong?"

"On one of them, I should've stuck it in there [harder]. I left it too high and the safety came in and made a good play. Another one, I tried to stick it into a 'stick' route and … " Bo caught himself. "Whatever," he said. "I've got to get better."

What he wanted to say was what he told me three days later: "On that stick route, I'm supposed to throw the ball as soon as I see Evan's numbers turn toward me. But it's based on coverage and where the defenders are. He ran the route too far and too close to the linebacker. I never saw the defender."

The press conference closed with a question about the importance of rallying in the second half and leaving the Georgia Dome with a win.

"Very important, especially going into Vandy [next week]. The momentum we're trying to establish here with our fan base and our team … it was real important."

Granted, the interceptions were alarming and they muddied how the win would be viewed. But only seven times in Ole Miss history had a quarterback thrown for more yards in a game than Bo's 387 in the Georgia Dome that evening. He had done it twice: 416 against Arkansas in 2013 and 403 against Vanderbilt in 2012.

• • •

Back in Oxford, the medical staff examined Bo's left shoulder.

"I have a sprained AC joint," Bo said the Sunday following the game.

"It's OK. It's nothing like the other shoulder when I hurt it my sophomore year."

What had him on edge before the game — Boise State possibly coming out in a defense they hadn't seen from the Broncos' coaches at prior stops during their careers — was never a huge issue.

"They did some things to try and take Laquon out of the game, but nothing really out of the ordinary," he said. "I've got to relax and remind myself that opponents aren't going to show much that I haven't seen.

"It was a strange game, one I can learn from going forward. And that's what I'll do. I'll be better because of it."

Bo said he was especially happy for Core, the 6-foot-3, 196-pound junior from Auburn, Alabama. He caught 4 passes for 110 yards and two touchdowns.

He did so with a lot on his mind, and even more on his heart.

His mother, Amy Core, died July 18 without warning of a brain aneurysm. She was 37 years old and a teacher in the Auburn city schools. She had earned undergraduate and Master's degrees in education at Troy University.

At church, she sang in the choir and taught Sunday School. Her obituary said she was a "God fearing woman" who "devoted herself to walking with God, while raising her children to do the same."

Cody Core spent his first two seasons splitting time between offense and defense while making his mark on the kickoff coverage team.

The coaches moved him to receiver prior to fall camp, and he found a home. He was consistent and made some 'jump ball' plays. He replaced Adeboyejo as the third starting receiver.

"We all told Cody we were there for him," Bo said. "He thanked us, but he never really wanted to talk about it. He has been pretty quiet about it. I can't imagine what he was going through during camp, and then scoring his first touchdown in Atlanta ... he seemed really happy after the game.

"And he's one of those guys that is gaining my trust as a receiver. He will go up and fight for the ball. And he's tough. He's not scared to go across the middle or catch a ball in traffic. And there aren't many guys on the field who can take one 76 yards to the end zone. He showed his speed.

"I know he is playing for his mom. That probably had a lot to do with how he came into camp and just took a starting position. He was obviously motivated."

. . .

I have my own Amy Core story.

Following a home game early in 2013, the walkway area in the south end zone at Vaught-Hemingway Stadium had nearly cleared while I sat in the stands and talked football with friends. As I walked onto the concourse, I passed a woman wearing a No. 88 jersey.

"Does Cody Core belong to you?" I asked.

She smiled. "Yes, he does."

"I just want to tell you that I really enjoy watching the way your son plays football. Everybody can learn a lesson watching the effort he plays with."

"Aw, thank you for saying that," she said. "I really appreciate it."

I remember she had a gentle spirit about her. And every word I told her was true. Even when his role was primarily on special teams, Cody Core played the game the proper way.

When I heard of her passing, I got chills remembering our 20-second exchange that night in Oxford. I was grateful to have met her.

Chapter 15

Two seasons and one game into his third as head coach at Ole Miss, we know this about Hugh Freeze: He will answer in detail just about any question a reporter throws at him.

None of this Bill Belichick "we're on to Cincinnati" or "we're trying to win the football game" crumbs. And no veering off the interstate when asked about a certain player's on-the-field mistakes the way Alabama's Nick Saban is prone to do. *"We ask our players to play with great effort, ah-ight? We expect and demand a lot of them. But they're going to make some mistakes because they're human, ah-ight? What I prefer to focus on is when a young man gets up after he's been knocked down, ah-ight?"*

That is not Freeze's style. He will talk about personnel and he will discuss injuries, openly and honestly.

At his Monday press conference, four days after the win over Boise State and five days before his team would open the SEC season against Vanderbilt in Nashville, he went into detail when asked again about Bo's three interceptions.

"He doesn't have freedom [to come off progressions]. The first one he threw is not even part of the progression. He didn't come off the progression. He threw it to a place that shouldn't be a part of the progression," Freeze said. "The second one, down in the end zone, was a combination, as it's a part of the progression, but it shouldn't have been his first look. The receiver had really bad spacing that called for one guy to guard two … the third one was a play we really liked in that situation. We ran it, and the backer made a good play and Bo didn't see him. That was where he should start his read. The other two weren't where the ball should go on his first read."

Later, he was asked about Bo's decision making. He responded: "Our relationship has matured, and I think I'm easier on him than I used to be, and maybe I shouldn't be, but I didn't think that was working, either. I think he was pressing the other night, and I'm hopeful that's over with and you'll see more like the second half when we didn't have any of that. I'm hopeful that will carry over.

"I'm not exasperated with him. Obviously, I was disappointed. I was disappointed for him. He wants to do better than anybody, and I'm not going to beat him up over it. The guy has done a lot of great things for us and played a really good second half the other night. We just have to keep coaching him and making sure on Thursday, like we always do, that he understands each package. If he doesn't understand it, then we don't carry it. It's his job then to make sure he goes out there and executes it. He didn't in the first half like we'd like to see, but you don't have to tell him that. He understands that. I hope its part of him pressing and maybe being too emotional or so ready to play again. I hope that's what it was."

Eventually, the conversation turned to Vanderbilt.

Yes, the Commodores had a new coach — Derek Mason, who spent 20 years as an assistant coach in college and the NFL and was fresh off a three-year stint as assistant head coach and defensive coordinator at Stanford.

He also was fresh off a 37-7 home loss to Temple in his Vanderbilt debut. The Commodores committed seven turnovers.

Mason replaced James Franklin, who took the job at Penn State in January. Franklin had made Vanderbilt relevant during his three seasons as head coach. He also had given Ole Miss fits. The Commodores beat the Rebels in 2011 and 2012 and led heading into the game's final minute-and-change in 2013.

Vandy had always been a thorn in Ole Miss' side, winning the first 19 times they played. Entering Saturday's contest, the Commodores had taken five of the past six meetings. In what has become one of Vanderbilt's biggest rivalry games, 10 of the last 15 games had been decided by eight points or fewer.

And the 2012 game in Oxford still stuck in the craws of a lot of Rebel players.

Fighting for a bowl berth with an overall record of 5-4, Ole Miss led 23-6 early in the third quarter, but the Commodores closed it to 23-20 entering the fourth. A 27-yard Bryson Rose field goal with 2:43 remaining gave Ole Miss a 26-20 lead.

But behind senior quarterback Jordan Rodgers — with his big brother Aaron, the Green Bay Packers' quarterback, watching from the sideline — Vandy moved 79 yards in nine plays to win, 27-26. Rodgers hit Chris Boyd on a 26-yard corner route in the end zone with 52 seconds remaining.

It should have never come to that — and wouldn't with the current replay rules in place. On the winning drive, facing fourth and 2 from the Vandy 46, Rodgers scrambled right for three yards and a first down — but replays clearly showed that he went down well short of the first down.

Ole Miss dropped to 5-5, and was forced to beat Mississippi State in the Egg Bowl to earn its bowl trip.

That wasn't lost on the Rebels. Neither was the fact that it took a 75-yard miracle touchdown run by Jeff Scott with 1:07 left to win 39-35 the year before.

"No one will ever know how close I came to pulling that ball out of Jeff's stomach and keeping it," Bo said of the option play. "The only reason I let him take it was that I thought he could get a few yards, then get out of bounds and save us a timeout. I couldn't see him once he went around end … then I saw him running free in the secondary, and I knew nobody was going to catch him."

Against Temple, Vandy looked nothing like the team that had won nine games each of the two previous seasons. The Commodores played three quarterbacks and gained just 54 yards rushing, fumbled four times, and threw three interceptions. It was 34-3 after three quarters.

Freeze assured reporters his players would not take Vandy lightly.

"It's an SEC game on the road," he said. "They have really good players, particularly on the defensive line, which is a good place to start in this league."

• • •

During his Monday meeting with reporters, Bo took ownership of the first-half blunders.

"In big-time games like we're about to get into, especially SEC games, you throw three [interceptions] in the first half and you're probably down by three scores … going forward, I know what I have to do."

The day before, Bo told me: "It was a strange first half. I hadn't been hit since last fall. Usually, after the first hit I'm good to go and the nerves go away. But they stayed with me for a while the other night. I just couldn't get relaxed.

"I thought we'd run the ball better than we did. We had a lot of MA's [missed assignments) up front. Boise gave us a lot of different looks and were doing some shifting and shouting 'move!' Plus, our linemen were thinking instead of reacting. Heck, it was the first game. All of that will improve over the next couple of weeks.

"Everybody in the world is down on them right now, so that's the last thing they need from me. I'm talking to them, pumping them up, letting them know I believe in them. The season is way more than one half or one game. It's a long season. A grind. I want to make sure we still cut up and have fun with each other. The offensive line will be fine."

• • •

Approximately three dozen friends and family members would travel from Pulaski to Nashville for the game at the Titan's LP Field. Vanderbilt chose to move the game from its campus stadium, which was strange considering that Ole Miss had won just twice in the last five trips to the Commodores' home field.

"This is a special opportunity for Commodore Nation to enjoy a great football game and have a great time downtown," Vandy athletic director David Williams said. "We have typically had outstanding games with Ole Miss, and with eight home games we thought moving this one off-campus will further create an electric, bowl-like atmosphere."

Ole Miss was thrilled with the decision.

"I love playing at the Titans' stadium," Bo said by phone the night before the game. "It's pretty cool that we played the Music City Bowl there, and now we're back there again for our first SEC game."

Bo isn't falling for the popular opinion that Vanderbilt's ship sailed when Franklin left town.

"I think our fans really believe we're going to go out there and blow them out," he said. "That is not how we are approaching this game. I think they're going to be tough defensively. They only gave up 380 yards or so last week, and their offense put the defense back on the field seven times. I know they've got good players because I've played against them. They're going to get better, and we always get their best shot."

He said his left shoulder was sore earlier in the week. "But it's fine."

"I just want us to go out there tomorrow and play our game, I want the offensive line to relax and let's see what we can do," he said. "Our defense showed last week what it's all about. They'll keep us in every game. We just have to help them and make some plays."

Chapter 16

He had preached it to his players all week, but Freeze took one more opportunity to do so in the locker room moments before the game.

He wasn't concerned with the stadium environment.

"We create our own environment," he said firmly. "On our sideline, within our family, we create our own aura. We create our own feelings. We create them together.

"Today, you get to experience what very few people in this world ever do, playing football at this level, in this conference. It is a conference opener … and you get to experience it on the field … in the battle. Do your part … let's take this thing back 1-0 in this conference. Take the fight to them early."

The Rebels did just that. And it wouldn't have mattered if they had played the game on Vanderbilt's campus or pulled up the pews and rumbled inside the Ryman Auditorium.

Ole Miss was focused, more athletic, and more physical. The game ended 41-3, the Rebels' largest margin of victory in an SEC game since the 45-0 scrubbing of Mississippi State in 2008.

It could have been much worse.

Ole Miss outgained Vandy 547 yards to 167, converted 10 of 15 third downs and never punted.

Bo completed 23 of 30 passes for 320 yards and one touchdown. He did not throw an interception. He also didn't play after I'Tavius Mathers' 2-

yard touchdown run made it 34-0 with 9:29 left in the third quarter.

"When I-Train scored, I looked at one of the Vandy defensive ends and he just had this blank look on his face," Bo said. "I told him, 'Man, y'all have quit.' He never said anything. He just kept that blank stare going."

Tight end Evan Engram caught 7 passes for 112 yards, and Core had another good game — 4 catches, 85 yards, and a 27-yard touchdown reception.

Vandy stuck with senior Stephen Rivers — younger brother of San Diego Chargers' quarterback Phillip Rivers — and he completed just 6 of 25 passes for 60 yards. Cliff Coleman picked off a pass early in the third quarter and returned it 39 yards for a touchdown.

The Rebels' secondary, fast and furious, knocked down nine passes. Sophomore tackle Robert Nkemdiche, who constantly faced double teams, had a sack and a tackle for loss.

"I'll give [the defense] a shutout. We had that fumble [by Kincade] down there [on the Ole Miss 5-yard line] and they held them to a field goal.

"I think our defense has a chance to be good."

Freeze was pleased with his quarterback.

"I couldn't tell you that it was the way we thought it would go coming in, but Bo did a good job reading his progressions," he said. "He managed us well."

SEC Network analyst Brock Huard, the former Washington Huskies quarterback who spent six seasons in the NFL, said of Bo: "Just tremendous rhythm from the very onset … He spread the ball around to multiple receivers. You know what I liked most was him checking down, throwing the ball away, avoiding the mistakes."

Bo was the same as he had been post-game after throwing three picks the previous week — not too up, not too down. He seldom displays what is simmering inside.

"I had fun. I'm glad a lot of family and friends got to come and experience it with me," he said. "I think we got better today. Winning that first conference game is so huge, especially when it comes on the road."

Every player who traveled played in the game. That included the true freshmen twins from Bassfield, A.J. and C.J. Moore. They are defensive athletes, able to play linebacker or in the secondary. They have earned their traveling stripes by playing "phenomenal" on special teams, according to Freeze.

They had become fan favorites, in large part from their segments on Ole Miss' weekly Emmy Award-winning half-hour weekly documentary, *The Season*. In the episode that aired the week of the Vandy game, the twins were shown during a phone conversation the night before the Boise State game with their father, who reinforced the family's motto: "We show up to show out."

Veteran players had been heard saying it, which had to make Freeze smile. Any coach will take an unforced blend of talented veterans and exuberant youth who also have skills.

It is the chemistry from which special seasons have been born.

Chapter 17

Simple math said Bo was playing at an elite level.

In the second half of the Boise State game and in the first half against Vanderbilt combined, Bo completed 33 of 48 passes (68.8 percent) for 488 yards, 4 touchdowns, no interceptions. For perspective, that would have set a school record for yards in a game.

"There is no question he's much more mature," Freeze said on the weekly SEC teleconference leading up to Saturday's home opener against Louisiana-Lafayette. "He never got rattled or showed any signs of being down. He just wanted to get the next possession going. He handled it well, and our team handled it well. We were all encouraging him. He's very resilient. To be a quarterback in this league and have some of the tough losses that you have sometimes and to get some of the criticism, you have to be resilient, and he's very much that."

Bo said there was a moment during the first half of the Vandy game when it was as if someone had given him the answer to a complicated math problem.

"I was feeling good, completing passes. I was relaxed and I was like, 'Yeah, *this* ... *this* is how you play quarterback. Don't force anything. Just keep getting first downs. Take the big play when it's there.' Playing quarterback is never easy, but you can make it easier by taking that approach.

"There was one play when I probably could have thrown one to Laquon in the end zone, but we were up 7-0. I didn't want to give them any momentum by throwing a pick. Laquon was like 'Come on, man, throw that thing up!' I said, 'Quon, you know I trust you. You know I want to get you the ball. But I'm not throwing an interception in that situation. You play receiver and I'll play quarterback.' He nodded and everything was cool. He knew I was right."

Bo laughed.

"Rod Taylor got in the game early," he said, referring to the highly recruited true freshman offensive lineman from Callaway High School in Jackson. "He is going to be really good. When we were changing ends of the field between the first and second quarter, Rod was walking down there and he goes, 'I promise to the Good Lord, I am so pumped right now. I'm playing SEC football in an NFL stadium.' It was so much fun watching that."

He said it was fun watching the Rebel defense hammer an SEC opponent, too.

Wommack's unit is allowing just 8 points per game, which ranks fifth nationally and second in the SEC. Opponents have only managed eight plays of 20 yards or longer.

"Coach Wommack is the best I've ever been around at making halftime adjustments," Bo said. "That's why the defense seems to always play better in the second half."

"We're getting pressure on the quarterback," Freeze said. "We have to continue to make sure we don't give up the big plays. I think our defense is talented enough that if people have to drive the length of the field consistently on us, we're going to win some of those battles."

Coleman, the senior cornerback from Lauderdale Lakes, Florida, was named SEC Defensive Player of the Week for his interception return for a touchdown.

The Rebels have five interceptions through two games. They had 13 in all of 2013.

• • •

Bo was realizing the responsibilities far from public view that go with being a senior quarterback.

On the Sunday following the Vanderbilt game, redshirt freshman running back Eugene Brazley sought Bo's advice in the locker room.

"What do I have to do to get on the field more?" he asked quietly.

Brazley, a 5-foot-9, 189-pound three-star recruit from New Orleans, was part of the blue chip-filled 2013 class. Nearly a year before signing day, he chose Ole Miss over Tennessee, Arizona State, and Houston. He suffered a torn ACL just before the start of 2013 fall camp but seems to have recovered nicely.

He showed quickness and elusiveness against Vanderbilt, gaining 34 yards on 6 carries. Only Jaylen Walton had more rushing yards — 35 on 8 carries. Freeze praised his cutback ability on the inside zone plays.

Bo said, "I told him, 'Just keep doing what you're doing. When you see the hole, hit it. And treat every practice like it's a game. You'll earn your game touches in practice.' He was rehabbing his knee last season, so he's only been in our offense really for six weeks or so. He doesn't understand all the [blitz] looks and [pass] protections yet. But he's got talent. And I like it when somebody is doing everything they can to get more playing time.

"It's like I told you in the summer, I see all these young guys busting their butts. They're seeing how the older guys do it, and they realize what's expected of them. Everybody gets along, everybody hangs out. Nobody is bringing a beef into the locker room about a girl or anything like that. Honestly, we don't have any shitheads on the team anymore. They either bought in to what Coach Freeze was saying, or they're gone. And I give him credit for that. You've got guys who probably hadn't bought in before — Cliff [Coleman], Bryon [Bennett], Senquez [Golson] — and they're leading now. And, honestly, I wasn't doing all that I could to lead the team the right way. I've had to be more vocal this year. Guys are really watching out for the team and for each other.

"You know, we didn't fly to Nashville. We took buses, instead. It's only four hours, but it's always a cool thing to fly. You know what? I was glad we didn't fly. It meant we wouldn't get back in time for guys to go out and party. Now, I probably wouldn't have been thinking that way the past two years. But I don't want anything to happen to this team.

"There was a back-to-school party last week, and I went around to each position group and told them, 'Do not show up at that party. Fights always break out at that thing.' Rod [Taylor] and Dayall [Harris] were like, 'Dang, this is a big party. We want to go.' But both of them told me later, 'When I got to thinking about it, I realized I wasn't thinking about you or the rest of my teammates when I was making that decision.' Both of them said they learned a lesson from that. And as far as I know, nobody on the team went.

"I'm telling you, man, I've never seen a team like this. Of course, we haven't had any adversity yet. Boise State was not adversity. I mean adversity like being down 14 points or 17 points to a really good team. How are we going to react? I think I know how, but you never really know until you go through it. At some point, we'll find out."

• • •

Freeze hoped his team, which moved up to No. 14 in the AP poll, was mature enough to handle the pitfalls that go with playing an out-matched opponent such as Louisiana-Lafayette.

"The bull's-eye on our chest this week will be huge," Freeze said. "We expect to get Lafayette's best shot."

That wasn't lip service. The Ragin' Cajuns, coached by Mississippi native Mark Hudspeth, had won nine games each of the three previous seasons and defeated Nevada, Tulane and East Carolina in consecutive bowl games. They shared the 2014 Sun Belt Conference title with Arkansas State.

"As soon as I saw our schedule, this game jumped out," Bo said. "I've been in the Sun Belt. I know how geared up they're going to be coming in here Saturday. I know I sound like Coach Freeze right now, but I remember when I was at Arkansas State and was like, 'Hell, yeah! We get to play Auburn this week!' That's how Sun Belt players look at these opportunities. They've got some players from Mississippi, too. A lot of those guys probably wanted to come here.

"I'm treating this just like any other game. I'm not going out and thinking I have to throw for a bunch of yards because this isn't an SEC opponent. I don't want to make mistakes and give the media the chance to start that Jekyll and Hyde stuff again."

Something even worse had started, something Bo would grow to despise. It was one of college football's hottest catch phrases: Good Bo, Bad Bo. The Good Bo throws touchdowns and the Bad Bo throws interceptions.

"I have no idea where that got started, but it pisses me off every time I hear it," he said. "I just have to keep playing good and make them stop talking about it."

• • •

Saturday's first home game meant his first Walk of Champions as a senior.

It is a single-file walk by players and coaches through The Grove, rated the No. 1 tailgating spot in all of college football by *The Sporting News*, then a winding path between a few academic buildings in an area known on game day as "Whiskey Alley." The final leg is across All American Drive, through a parking lot and into Vaught-Hemingway Stadium. Fans form a raucous tunnel the entire length of the walk two hours, 15 minutes before the game. "The first few times, it's really cool," Bo said. "Now, I've done it so many times I kind of take it for granted. I need to enjoy every step. Really soak it in. I've only got seven of these left."

Chapter 18

There was a time not so long ago when Vaught-Hemingway Stadium could hardly be classified as rowdy. Touchdowns were greeted with polite applause. Fans dressed as if they were going to a reception at the Governor's mansion. Many returned to their tents, televisions and toddies in The Grove before the fourth quarter.

This has been the site of greatness. Ole Miss was awarded three national championships and won six SEC titles under Coach John Vaught during a stretch from 1947 to 1963. The 1959 team, with a first-string defense that allowed just three points all season, was voted the SEC Team of the Decade. Many argue it ranks with the best of all time.

For a brief period, from 1968 through 1970, a lanky quarterback from Drew High School pushed Ole Miss back into the limelight. Archie Manning helped the Rebels win 22 games and a Sugar Bowl and became a legend doing so. He finished third in the 1970 Heisman Trophy voting even though he suffered a broken arm in the season's seventh game.

It would be 33 years before Ole Miss returned to the national stage, when Archie and Olivia Manning's' youngest son, Eli, was the senior quarterback.

Forty years after the Rebels' last conference title, LSU traveled to Oxford on November 22, 2003 with the SEC West Division championship on the line.

Vaught-Hemingway rocked like never before. The newly enclosed south end zone, sporting three decks of seats and suites, made it larger and louder. Starving for their school to be great again, fans screamed and cheered and found it perfectly acceptable to attend games wearing jerseys sporting the No. 10 — Eli's number.

LSU, coached by Nick Saban, defeated Ole Miss, 17-14, and went on to win the national championship.

Still, fans and the University got a taste of how it used to be, and what could be again. Vaught-Hemingway adopted a new personality during that game, which started at mid-afternoon and unfolded under a sky painted violet — a color born of red and blue.

• • •

As the national anthem was performed moments before the Rebels would battle Louisiana-Lafayette, Freeze's team gathered silently in the tunnel, out of sight of the fans.

The players wore Navy blue jerseys, pants and headgear. They remained silent as they moved closer to the tunnel exit.

A sellout crowd of 60,937, row by row, interlocked arms and swayed left and right to the blaring beat of Sean "Puff Daddy" Combs' 1998 rap song *Come With Me*, featuring the driving riff of Led Zeppelin's hit *Kashmir*.

"Locking the Vaught" had become a fun, emotional ritual for fans during the Freeze era.

Soon, the players were swaying along with them. But they did so with somber hearts.

Stan Sandroni, the longtime sideline reporter for the Ole Miss football radio team, died Wednesday night of a heart attack at the age of 64. The players knew him, had traveled to games with him, and been interviewed by him.

Just before leaving the locker room, Freeze told them: "You have the opportunity today that very few people have. Don't waste it. We've been reminded this week that life is very short. And we lay in our bed at night and we think 'Did I do everything that I could do today to make sure we were successful?' ... Stan Sandroni? He got that. He loved this program. He spent 26 years serving it. Life is short, men."

Louisiana-Lafayette had no chance.

Bo completed his first 14 pass attempts, including touchdown strikes to Vince Sanders of 14 and 24 yards and another to Jaylen Walton for 40 yards. I'Tavius Mathers ran 56 yards for a score. The Rebels led 28-6 at halftime.

Bo threw another touchdown pass, 13 yards to Cody Core, on the first possession of the third quarter. Senquez Golson intercepted his second pass of the game and returned it 59 yards for a score. Walton ran 71 yards for a touchdown to make it 49-13 entering the fourth quarter.

Freeze and Werner used 290-pound tight Jeremy Liggins as the "wildcat" quarterback, and he thundered in for a 2-yard touchdown.

Final score: Ole Miss 56, UL-L 15.

The offense rolled up 554 yards, including a 214-yard day on the ground. Walton rushed for 89 yards on 7 carries. Mathers gained 57 on just 3 rushes. "I've said it before and I'll say it again," Bo said. "If we can have some success running the football, nobody can stop us. It puts defenses in too big of a bind with the weapons we have at receiver."

It was a career day for senior wideout Vince Sanders, the former four-star recruit out of Noxubee County High School in Macon. He caught 8 passes for 125 yards and the two scores, flashing his signature "you can't see me" wave in front of his face after each score.

"I've told anyone who would listen how good Vince is," Bo said. "He is so reliable. He is the same guy week in, week out. I remember last year, people were talking about our 'big three' at receiver — Laquon, Evan and [Donte] Moncrief. I would always say, 'Don't forget about Vince.' He's kind of a quiet guy and maybe that's why he goes unnoticed. But he has made play after play since I've been here. I trust him as much as any receiver we have."

Once again, the defense was stinging and stingy. UL-L managed 322 total yards, 193 on the ground.

Postgame, Hudspeth said Ole Miss has "one of the best defensive lines in the nation."

The secondary wasn't too shabby, either. In three games, Ole Miss had picked off 8 passes. Golson already had three — half as many as he had the previous three seasons combined.

Freeze had openly said there were times when he wasn't sure Golson would "make it" in his program. While not considered a bad guy, Golson had always marched to his own beat.

He was different this season. "It's very rewarding to see good things happen because a kid really decides to buy in," Freeze said.

Golson came close to never playing a game at Ole Miss. He was drafted in the eighth round of the Major League Baseball draft out of Pascagoula High School by the Boston Red Sox. He would have been picked sooner, but baseball teams knew there was a good chance he would play college football.

Red Sox scouts believed he had a huge "up" side as an outfielder and club officials were determined to sign him. Following a preseason scrimmage at Ole Miss on August 13, 2011, Golson talked with Red Sox representatives in Oxford and then flew to Boston. The deadline for prospects to sign with the Major League club that selected them was August 15, a Monday, by midnight Eastern time.

Reports said the Red Sox offered him $1.3 million.

"It was more than that," Golson told me. "They came in with more money right near the end. And, trust me, I knew that was a *lot* of money. I had just turned eighteen.

"I'll never forget, I had the pen in my hand and ready to sign. But something wouldn't let me do it. Every time I started to sign my name on that line, something would pull my hand away. I can't explain it. But I knew it was God's way of telling me not to sign."

During his freshman season, Golson became a regular on ESPN's college highlights. Alabama's Trent Richardson faked him to the Vaught-Hemingway turf on a touchdown run. The play was shown over and over during Richardson's failed race for the Heisman Trophy.

Golson was providing a new set of highlights.

"I love my teammates and my coaches," he said. "I think we can be special."

. . .

As for Bo, Freeze called his performance against UL-L "solid."

The new "solid" in Oxford was completing 23 of 28 passes for 316 yards, four touchdowns and one interception. Freeze pulled him midway of the third quarter, not wanting to risk injury.

For the season, Bo was 71 of 94 (76 percent, best in the SEC), 1,023 yards, 9 touchdowns, 4 interceptions.

Post-game, he was asked about his throwing shoulder.

"It's definitely 100 percent. It feels great. I definitely feel stronger than I did a year ago."

We talked for a few minutes after the press conference. I asked his emotions concerning the death of Stan Sandroni.

"I loved how much he cared about us and how invested he was in us doing well," Bo said. "He would've liked that game today."

Remember Terrance Broadway, the other quarterback EMCC was recruiting when O'Conner approached Coach Buddy Stephens about possibly signing Bo?

Broadway played quarterback for UL-L. He was never sacked but took countless hits from the Rebels' pass rush. He completed 15 of 30 passes for 129 yards, no touchdowns, 3 interceptions. UL-L dropped to 0-2.

Meanwhile, Ole Miss improved to 3-0 with a bye week coming up. And the hype about Alabama's trip to Oxford on Oct. 4 was about to begin.

But following their bye, the Rebels had another non-conference opponent to play before Alabama — Memphis on Sept. 27 in Oxford.

The players and coaches knew that game would be no small hurdle.

Chapter 19

On the Saturday of Ole Miss' off week, Bo spent the day at his apartment in Oxford watching SEC football.

I sent him a text at halftime of the 2:30 p.m. game between Florida and Alabama but didn't hear back until early that evening.

Me: You pulling for Florida? Or don't care?

Bo: Nah, I want Bama #2 when we beat them. I'm about to throw up watching this damn state game

He got his wish in the contest played in Tuscaloosa: Alabama 42, Florida 21.

But his disdain for the way the Mississippi State-LSU game was going in Baton Rouge only got worse. State led 17-3 at halftime and 34-10 early in the fourth quarter. State eventually won 34-29, but the score doesn't indicate how badly the Bulldogs pounded LSU. The Tigers scored on two long passes in the final two minutes to make the score respectable.

State ran around and through eighth-ranked LSU for 302 yards and gained 570 overall. Dak Prescott put on a show, rushing 22 times for 105 yards and throwing for 268. He accounted for three touchdowns.

The Bulldogs entered the game 3-0 and unranked because their three victories were against Southern Mississippi, University of Alabama-Birmingham, and South Alabama.

But they were certain to crash the poll party. The only question: How high would they go?

• • •

The University of Memphis — formerly Memphis State —is often an unnerving opponent for Ole Miss. It's a little to gain and a whole lot to lose proposition.

It had never been truer as the Rebels prepared for the Tigers to invade Vaught-Hemingway for a 6 p.m. kickoff on Saturday.

With only 80 miles separating the schools, it is a natural rivalry. Ole Miss considers the Memphis area crucial in recruiting. And there is the obvious scenario of the mighty SEC vs. the American Athletic Conference.

After routing Austin Peay 63-0 opening week, the Tigers traveled to the Rose Bowl in Pasadena, California and played 11th-ranked UCLA to the wire. They lost, 42-35, but sophomore quarterback Paxton Lynch threw for 305 yards and a touchdown. They piled up 469 yards of total offense. The difference in the game was UCLA's Heisman Trophy candidate — quarterback Brett Hundley. He passed for 396 yards and three touchdowns.

Still, the Tigers' defense was ranked in the Top 15 nationally in sacks and tackles for loss. And Coach Justin Fuente's team certainly left the West Coast confident they could play with anyone.

Meaningful games weren't new to Fuente, who was in his third season at Memphis. He was an assistant coach for five seasons at TCU — the final three as co-offensive coordinator and quarterbacks coach. He was part of TCU's undefeated 2010 season, which included a Rose Bowl victory over Wisconsin.

The Tigers were 4-8 in his Fuente's first year as head coach, but he rallied them in 2013 to a 9-3 record, a share of the AAC title and a No. 25 ranking in the final AP poll.

This wouldn't be an easy week for Ole Miss to play any opponent, with Alabama looming. But the fact that it was Memphis coming to town only complicated the situation.

"Coach Freeze has already talked to us about it," Bo said Sunday night. "And the leaders — me and Cody and C.J. — are all reminding the other players that the Memphis game means everything. We've seen them on tape, and they got our attention. They obviously have some talent the way they played UCLA."

• • •

Just as Freeze headed to his Monday press conference, there was news out of New York: CBS announced it would televise the Ole Miss-Alabama game on October 4th in the coveted 2:30 p.m. Central time slot.

It was always a good thing to be part of the featured SEC game of the week, which the CBS telecast has been considered for years. Freeze viewed it as a great recruiting opportunity.

But right now, he viewed it as a distraction. All he could do was keep his own words and actions geared toward Memphis and hope his players — and the media, if possible — followed suit.

"Athleticism," Freeze answered when asked what stood out about Memphis. "Their quarterback is playing really well. Defensively, they're very aggressive. They tackle extremely well. They get off the field on third down … if their quarterback keeps playing solid, their defense is good enough to keep them in every game."

• • •

Freeze had a surprise at Tuesday's team meeting.

He opened a box and pulled out a powder blue Ole Miss helmet with a single red stripe down the middle and a gray facemask. It had been the Rebels' chosen helmet from 1948 through 1977 and from 1983 through 1994.

The players were quiet for a few seconds.

"We were shocked," Treadwell said.

Then they went nuts.

"Loved it," Bo said. "It was just something different. It looked good.

"We knew some fans had been wanting Ole Miss to switch back to the powder blue helmets, or at least wear them one game a season."

Ken Crain's equipment staff had to fit the players, then add a stripe and the Ole Miss logo and attach facemasks, visors, and other decals.

The biggest problem was keeping anyone other than the players and staff from finding out before Saturday.

"Coach Freeze told us, 'You can't tell *anyone*. And we're going to have to practice in the Manning Center,'" Bo said.

Practices were closed to the media, even the bits they were usually permitted to watch on Wednesday. Black curtains were placed over the glass doors and windows during workouts.

"We had to practice in the helmets," Bo explained. "You didn't want to put a helmet on for a game that you hadn't worn and gotten used to wearing. The change in color didn't bother me as far as looking at receivers and stuff like that. It was just so crazy around the facility.

"I had someone who runs track ask me 'What's going on in the Manning Center? They wouldn't let us in.' I said, 'I have no idea what that's about.' It was hard keeping it from everybody."

This was much more than a motivational trick.

Before the season, Ole Miss athletic director Ross Bjork had designated this Chucky Mullins Week. Among the ways Ole Miss planned to honor its fallen hero was changing Coliseum Drive to Chucky Mullins Drive. And the team would wear the powder blue helmets, which Chucky wore.

Chucky was paralyzed while delivering a jarring hit to the back of a Vanderbilt receiver in 1989 at Vaught-Hemingway. Four vertebrae in his neck were crushed. He died in 1991 due to complications from the injury.

ESPN aired the documentary, *It's Time*, on September 4th, telling the story of Chucky and the friendship that developed between Chucky and the Vanderbilt player he struck, running back and tight end Brad Gaines. Death did not end their friendship.

Gaines, who has made a good living in the business world, travels three times a year to Chucky's grave — the anniversary of the injury, the anniversary of Chucky's death and Christmas Day. He drives the three hours from Gallatin, Tennessee to Russellville, Alabama alone. His wife and children have come to understand it is something Gaines feels he must do, and wants to do. Gaines often attends Ole Miss games.

He would be at Vaught-Hemingway rooting for the Rebels against Memphis.

• • •

After practice Thursday, Bo and a friend from high school drove 75 minutes from Oxford to Fulton, where EMCC was playing Itawamba.

"It was 51-0 when I left, and I saw the teams get into a pretty good fight," Bo said and laughed during the drive back to Oxford. "It was good to see Coach Stephens and some other guys. They're good again. They've got athletes all over the field. I stood down on the sidelines with them. It was fun."

I asked him if he was truly concerned about Memphis.

"I am," he said. "Their defensive coordinator is really good. You never know where the blitz is coming from. They're not like most teams. Usually, if you go to the line of scrimmage and see a safety rolled down or a safety stacked on top of the tight end, the blitz is coming from that side. With Memphis, it's just as likely to come from the other side.

"It's hard to pick up any tendencies. I'm hoping when I'm actually on the field with them, I can pick up something that will tip where the blitz is coming from. It never fails that you can pick up things that you just can't see on film. It might be an edge rusher leaning back just a little bit, meaning he's dropping into coverage. Or just the way a player stands. Which foot is forward? Is he fidgety? That's the sort of stuff you can only see once you get out there across from them.

"But I have to call the right protection on third down, and the guys have to execute it. Jaylen and I'Tavius are going to have to be really good at picking up the blitz. If we can do that, we can make some plays."

Bo said his mind hadn't wandered toward Alabama.

"I'm too busy trying to figure out Memphis," said. "Plus, Coach Freeze is doing a really good job of putting up quotes from some of the Memphis players about how much this game means to them.

"Oh, by the way. We're going to have a real cool surprise for everybody Saturday," Bo said.

"There is a rumor that y'all are coming out in powder blue helmets," I said, repeating what I had read on some Internet message boards.

"Naw, nothing that drastic," Bo said. "We're undefeated in our Navy blue helmets. Coach Freeze is too superstitious to change headgear. But what we have planned is cool. The fans will get a kick out of it."

. . .

Sure enough, the Rebels were not wearing powder blue helmets when they came out for warm-ups. Bo, Prewitt, Denny and C.J. Johnson were wearing their regular helmets when they walked out as captains a few minutes before the rest of the team.

Freeze and crew kept the cover up going all the way through the coin toss, when the team finally exited the tunnel wearing the powder blues. Equipment managers had the four captains' helmets, plus a powder blue undershirt for Bo, hidden on the sidelines.

The 61,291 fans, many of them wearing "38 Chucky Mullins" buttons that were handed out upon entering the stadium, roared for their unbeaten warriors and for the appearance of the throwback helmets.

They roared again just three minutes into the game when Bo faked a handoff, rolled right and passed to Treadwell, who was running a post from the left side. Wide open. Perfect pass. Sixty-three yard touchdown to go up 7-0.

That would be the Rebels' only score until the fourth quarter.

Bo threw two interceptions and fumbled once when the pocket collapsed around him. Ole Miss rushed for just 109 yards through three quarters.

And freshman kicker, Gary Wunderlich, was ejected after a fight broke out on the kickoff following the Treadwell touchdown.

While the offense struggled and tempers were on edge, the Ole Miss defense was relentless and dominant. Memphis converted 1 of 11 first downs in the first three periods and could muster only a 40-yard field goal in the first quarter.

Every good team has games like Ole Miss was experiencing against the Tigers. But good teams on their way to being great find a way to close things out in the fourth quarter.

Freeze's team did that.

Andrew Fletcher kicked a 19-yard field goal, Walton raced 23 yards for a touchdown and, for good measure, Bo passed 17 yards to Treadwell with 1:18 left. Ole Miss won, 24-3, on Freeze's 45th birthday.

"Chucky would have been proud of the helmets, the baby blues, and particularly how the defense played," Freeze said. "I know Chucky would have loved that."

"I don't know if we have had a better defensive effort than that in our two and a half years here. They were really phenomenal. [Memphis] was a team putting up some really good numbers."

"We were flying around, doing our job, being in the right place at the right time, and making the plays we're supposed to make," said junior linebacker Denzel Nkemdiche. "This is probably the most emotional we have played since we have been here. That's us now. That's who we are. We have seen what we can do. We have seen how our defense is coming together."

So had Memphis.

"They kicked our tail," Fuente said. "They didn't do anything new, they're just pretty darn good."

Ole Miss held the Tigers to 104 yards total offense, including 23 yards on 31 rushes. Toss out a 42-yard pass in the first period, and the Tigers managed 62 yards on 61 plays. Lynch completed 13 of 31 passes for 81 yards and was sacked four times.

Fittingly, sixth-year senior linebacker D.T. Shackelford — a second-time winner of the Chucky Mullins Courage Award, and wearing Chucky's No. 38 jersey — led Ole Miss with eight tackles. Conner had seven. Denzel Nkemdiche and Mike Hilton each made six stops and had two tackles for loss. The sacks came from Lavon Hooks, Johnson, Haynes, and Bennett.

Trae Elston nabbed his first interception of the season, and the quick-as-a-cat nose tackle, Isaac Gross, recovered a fumble.

Offensively, the Rebels weren't sharp.

"Give credit to Memphis. They had a lot to do with that," Bo said. "That defensive coordinator [Barry Odom] is the best I've ever gone against in my time here. They really did a good job.

"But I can't fumble and I can't throw picks, no matter what the defense is doing."

Bo finished 22 of 37 for 248 yards, two touchdowns. Walton had his best game so far, rushing for 78 yards on 10 carries.

And Laquon Treadwell finally had a breakout game — 5 catches, 123 yards, two scores.

Many credit Treadwell, the 6-foot-2, 230-pound sophomore who grew up in Crete, Illinois, for kick-starting Ole Miss on its way to signing the 2013 class. He was rated the No. 1 receiving prospect in the country by most recruiting services and headed to the University of Michigan. A close family friend happened to be traveling through Mississippi and decided to detour off I-55 and take a glance at Ole Miss' campus. He and his family were blown away by its beauty and encouraged Treadwell to take an official visit to Oxford.

With offers from every school imaginable, Treadwell visited December 1, 2012 and committed January 17.

Treadwell had always been one of those guys other players want to be around. He immediately became one of the Rebels' hardest-working recruiters.

"He is a great guy on and off the field," Bo said. "The older players respect the heck out of him, and the younger players want to be just like him. He's easy going, always positive. But he is a monster on the field. I've never seen a receiver block like he does — and enjoy blocking as much as he does. And he will battle for a football like nobody I've been around. He and I have built a special bond. We can almost read each other's minds on the field.

"I remember during his first preseason camp, though, I wasn't sure he was everything I'd heard about. He was good, but I kept asking 'Are y'all sure he was the No. 1 receiver in the nation?' But, man, when that first game rolled around [against Vanderbilt], he was unbelievable. The one-handed catch that he made in the second half, where he just snatched the ball out of the air, was one of the best I've ever seen."

• • •

Finally, Freeze could exhale. It was officially Alabama week.

"I'm so glad this is over and everyone can do whatever talking they want to do about next week," Freeze said.

One of the first up: Cody Prewitt, the senior from Bay Springs who had never been one to mince words.

"They are coming into our house so we are not going to be intimidated," he said. "They are going to be the ones climbing up the hill."

Chapter 20

No matter how hard the press tried, Bo wasn't going to say anything that might be twisted into a negative comment about Alabama.

He learned his lesson in 2013. When asked on Monday before the game how he felt about the Ole Miss offense going against the Crimson Tide's defense, Bo answered: "I feel like we can put up points on anybody."

The comment became headlines and the focus of radio talk shows. Alabama fans were outraged.

"What was I supposed to say? That I'm just honored to be on the same field with Alabama?" Bo said the Monday after the Memphis game. "I would hope that every quarterback in the country feels like his offense can put up points on anybody. If I'd said the same thing about another school, it would have been no big deal. But when it's Alabama, everything is different. Their fans and their media get bent out of shape about the smallest things."

They took great pleasure in Alabama's shutout, 25-0, but a lot of Ole Miss fans said the defensive effort deserved an asterisk.

During the fourth quarter of the telecast, ESPN's cameras showed an Alabama coach — a coach whose duties were off the field —standing inside the coaches' booth in the press box. He was looking at the field through binoculars and talking with the other coaches while Ole Miss had the ball.

This wasn't just any coach. It was Tyler Siskey, whom Freeze hired as recruiting coordinator when he took the Ole Miss job. Siskey also coached two years with Freeze at Arkansas State.

Saban hired Siskey as associate director of player personnel in 2013 — one month after Ole Miss signed its greatest recruiting class in school history.

Said ESPN analyst Todd Blackledge when Siskey was shown peering through binoculars: "Alabama has really been locked in on what Ole Miss has tried to do offensively. They haven't been fooled by much of anything. Again, I go back to Tyler Siskey being on the Alabama staff. [He] spent those years with Hugh Freeze. Even though he's not coaching on the field, he was very involved this week in helping to prepare the Alabama defense."

Saban denied Siskey supplied any information during the game.

"He didn't really assist in the game plan, and he wasn't on a headset," Saban said when asked whether it was common for a non-coaching staff member to assist during a game. "He didn't talk to anybody during the game. I don't know if there's any rule that says he can't go into the press box and watch the games. And he wasn't in any different position than he's ever been in a game."

There is an NCAA rule, 11.7.2, that says a team can only have one head coach, nine assistants, and four graduate assistants who can coach during a game.

When Siskey accepted the job, Alabama quarterback A.J. McCarron was asked how it would affect him in 2013. Siskey was McCarron's offensive coordinator in high school.

"None playing-wise," McCarron answered. "He's in recruiting or whatever he's doing."

So if Siskey had nothing to do with the team "playing-wise" why was he in the coaches' booth?

Freeze played the issue down the middle.

"I don't know where [Siskey] typically is [during games]," Freeze said on Monday following the game. "Certainly, I'll say that Alabama had a wonderful defensive plan for us." There was more than a dab of sarcasm in his voice.

But Freeze quickly added: "I give them a lot of credit for the work that they put in in preparing for us, whether it was in the summertime or just in the week. Nick [Saban] and Kirby [Smart] are two of the best in the business. Not that they need a lot of help in preparing a game plan, but I'm sure Siskey helped in some way. Tyler Siskey is a good man. I hate that it's been quite the drama. Did I feel like they had an excellent plan? For whatever reason, I did."

He added: "They're good. They played with an edge and a little attitude Saturday night."

In December 2013, I asked Bo if he believed Siskey made any difference in the game.

"No doubt in my mind he did," he said. "They seemed to always have the perfect [defensive] play call for what we were doing. Whether it was by personnel or whatever, he was able to tell the defensive staff whether it was going to be a run or pass. If a defense can narrow it down to that, it makes a huge difference in the calls a defensive coordinator can make. And it only takes a couple of seconds to get that information to the sidelines and then out to the players on the field."

When I brought up the subject the week of the upcoming Alabama game, Bo was hesitant to discuss it.

"You already know what I think," he said. "I'd rather not say anything else about it."

But know this: The situation ate at him. Ole Miss only gained 205 yards. Bo was 17 of 31 for 159 yards, no touchdowns, no interceptions.

He called it "the most frustrating game" of the 2013 season.

Chapter 21

Finally, ESPN's *College GameDay* was coming to Oxford.

Host Chris Fowler and analysts Kirk Herbstreit, Lee Corso, Desmond Howard, David Pollack, and Samantha Ponder would set up shop Saturday in The Grove from 8 a.m. to 11 a.m.

The show offers profiles of coaches and players around the country, takes a look at the day's matchups, and in the final segment a celebrity associated with the host school serves as a "guest picker" as Corso and the crew predict the winners of the top games. Fans are encouraged to stand behind the set and cheer, chant, and boo while holding up homemade signs.

GameDay first aired in 1987. ESPN began taking the show on the road to college campuses in 1993. Usually, it was the site of what was considered to be game of the week.

During those two decades, *GameDay* made 13 trips to Ohio State and 12 to Florida. It visited Bowling Green and North Dakota State.

It went to Vanderbilt and Kentucky.

As of the final weekend in September 2014, it had camped at every SEC school except for two: Ole Miss and Mississippi State.

Ole Miss fans were especially irritated because *GameDay* and The Grove seemed like the perfect marriage. Instead of choosing to visit Oxford for the 2003 Ole Miss–LSU game, which would decide the SEC West, *GameDay* went to Ann Arbor, Michigan, site of the matchup between No. 4 Ohio State and No. 5 Michigan.

For Freeze, such exposure was just another toy in the recruiting toolbox. Millions would get a next-best-thing-to-being-there look at Ole Miss' program and campus.

"That's going to provide a very festive atmosphere here in Oxford," Freeze said at his Monday press conference, "and we're excited to showcase our atmosphere in the Grove."

A hot topic concerned who would represent the Rebels as guest picker. Conversations centered on someone from the Manning family or perhaps former New Orleans Saints running back Deuce McAllister.

But Ole Miss' energetic and aggressive athletic director, Ross Bjork, was thinking way outside the box. If his plan worked out, young people who had never watched a football game or heard of Ole Miss would be in front of their televisions on Saturday.

• • •

The latest Associated Press poll had Ole Miss No. 11 and Alabama No. 3. But the *USA Today* coaches' poll ranked the Crimson Tide No. 1. Mississippi State entered the AP poll at No. 12.

Ole Miss was 0-10 when facing the nation's top-ranked team, and its record against Alabama was more than underwhelming: 10-42-2.

The most recent win over Alabama was in 2003, Eli's senior season. Bo was 11 years old.

This Alabama team hadn't been shown the respect by the media that a typical Saban team receives. McCarron had started at quarterback for three seasons and won two national championships. He graduated. His replacement, Blake Sims, was a barely-used fifth-year senior who played running back early in his Alabama career.

Still, this was Alabama. Saban's previous five recruiting classes were ranked first, fourth, second, seventh, and fourth nationally by Scout. Ole Miss' heralded 2013 class was rated 10th by Scout, six spots behind Alabama. Saban's team was coming to Oxford 4-0, having beaten West Virginia, 33-

23; Florida Atlantic, 41-0; Southern Mississippi, 52-14; and Florida, 42-21. And Sims had played well. In Alabama's last game, two weeks before against Florida, he was 23 of 33 for 445 yards, 4 touchdowns, 1 interception. It was the second-most passing yards in Alabama history.

Senior wide receiver Amari Cooper, with sure hands and the speed to get deep, entered the game leading the nation with 43 catches for 655 yards and 5 touchdowns.

But there were a few statistics that gave the Rebels hope. Alabama had been penalized seven more times than its opponents and had lost five fumbles — foreign behavior for Saban-coached teams. Ole Miss' defense led the nation with 9 interceptions and had allowed only two touchdowns through four games. And this would be Alabama's — and Blake Sims' — first game on an opponent's campus. The opening win over West Virginia was at a neutral site, Atlanta's Georgia Dome.

"At the end of the day, it's about players playing their individual matchups and that's something we'll challenge our kids all week long to prepare themselves to do," Freeze said. "Looking back to the Memphis game, I'm really proud of our defense and the way they played. They made very few mental mistakes. We tackled extremely well and got turnovers and sudden-change moments."

It was mentioned by a reporter that just three years earlier, Ole Miss was going through a 2-10 season in which it lost all eight SEC games.

"That's a great point," Freeze said, "and I hope everyone understands that because I really want our people to enjoy the journey. I think it's human nature for all of us to get a bit head-in-the-clouds with all of what's going on right now. We all want that.

"But I sat back with my staff this morning and reminded coaches exactly what the process has been like with our journey to get us to this point. It certainly happened faster than I thought possible when we first got here.

"I'm going to enjoy this week. Last week, I have to be candid, it wasn't enjoyable for me."

Freeze was asked about Bo facing Alabama again.

"His mindset never changes," he said. "He'll be as confident as any kid on the field entering Saturday's game. He's always that way. It's a really good quality about him. He's very resilient. He'll be looking forward to this game."

The biggest injury concern, Freeze noted, was Senquez Golson with a tight hamstring. "He didn't play the last quarter and a half against Memphis," he said.

• • •

An interesting "family battle" would take place every time Alabama had the ball. Calling the Tide's plays was offensive coordinator Lane Kiffin. Coaching the Rebels' defensive front was his younger brother, Chris Kiffin.

Their dad, Monte, was a longtime NFL defensive coordinator who won a Super Bowl with the Tampa Bay Buccaneers.

Lane Kiffin was also the Tennessee head coach who showed no interest in signing Bo out of high school, although he bolted before signing day for the job at USC.

Lane Kiffin's only visit to Vaught-Hemingway occurred during his one season [2009] as the Vols' head coach. Dexter McCluster set an Ole Miss single-game rushing record with 282 yards and scored four touchdowns in a 41-17 blowout.

• • •

The secret was out two days before the game.

Ole Miss had recruited Katy Perry to be its guest picker for *GameDay*.

At the age of 29, Perry — a singer-songwriter — already was one of the best-selling artists in music history. At 25, she became the first female to have five songs off the same album — *Teenage Dreams* — go to No. 1 on the U.S. pop charts.

She had been unpredictable musically and personally, which fueled her popularity. When it came to business, she was the no-nonsense type. She earned $39 million in 2013, according to *Forbes*.

Perry's manager, Bradford Cobb, and her mentor, Glen Ballard, graduated from Ole Miss.

"She's actually wanted to come to a game for sometime now," Cobb said. "It just worked out time-wise."

Near the end of a grueling U.S. tour, Perry's calendar was clear on Saturday before playing a Sunday night show in Memphis.

Ole Miss, Oxford, the game, the football team, The Square, The Grove, … all of them were about to be part of a social media explosion like never before seen in Mississippi. Perry had 58 million Twitter followers, more than anyone in the world.

A week brimming with hype had just gone to another level.

· · ·

At 8:45 p.m., on the eve of the most important college game he had ever played, Bo sounded focused and confident.

"We just got out of our meeting," he said. "It was different than any I've been in since coming to Ole Miss. Coach Freeze was different.

"He's usually like, 'Let's go pick a fight, play for 60 minutes and then look at the scoreboard.' But none of that tonight. He told us, 'You're good enough to beat Alabama. You don't need a miracle. You don't need a bunch of crazy things to happen for us to win. I never imagined I'd be saying that in year three of our journey, but you can beat them.'

"There was a feeling in the room that the players believed it, too. And I think hearing it from Coach Freeze gave us a huge boost. He's always been straight with us. So for him to say it, he must believe it, too."

Bo met mid-afternoon with the CBS broadcast team of Verne Lundquist, Gary Danielson, and Allie LaForce.

"It was loose and relaxed, a lot more fun than going into the team room [for weekly press conferences]," he said. "They just said, 'No disrespect meant toward Ole Miss, but y'all have always been the 'other' team when we did y'all's games,'" Bo said. "I said, 'We've always been able to hang with Alabama, but now we have a great team and match up athlete for athlete.'"

"I knew whatever I said was probably going to be repeated on air, but I'm OK with that."

The only time Bo became aggravated was when they brought up "Good Bo, Bad Bo."

"I told them, 'I must be the only quarterback in the country who has thrown an interception.' But that's their job, to ask the questions."

There was no doubt in Bo's mind that "our defense is going to play lights out — just watch and see."

Bo said Freeze and the offensive staff "came up with a great game plan."

"Alabama is going to play us man [to man] coverage," he said. "That's what they feel comfortable doing. That's who they are, and they won't change for us. If they do, I think we can beat them. We have better athletes outside than they do."

Bo raved about Alabama's defensive front. "They're really, really good, just like they always are."

I asked if the defense's back seven were as talented as they had been in recent years.

"Nowhere close," he said.

Bo said he would probably run the football more than usual.

"We need at least 100 yards rushing so we can have some balance," he said. "It's time for me to start throwing my body around and taking some hits if I have to. I'll slide when the opportunity comes but I can't worry about that right now.

"And I can assure you of one thing: I will not throw an interception. If they're going to beat us, they'll have to find some other way."

Chapter 22

Most college games are scheduled years in advance: The dates and sites are usually set, then the TV networks decide the game times.

But when Texas A&M and Missouri joined the SEC in 2012, efforts to bridge them into the league's schedule became a nightmare. It forced some changes in 2013 game sites. Ole Miss was sent to Tuscaloosa for a second consecutive year. Rebel athletic officials were not happy. Having Alabama on the home schedule almost guarantees more season ticket sales.

But what a stroke of fortune the switch turned out to be.

On this first Saturday in October, the Rebels were playing at home instead of Tuscaloosa — and much better armed than in 2013 to take advantage of the opportunity in front of them.

The impact players from the 2013 signing class were bigger, faster, and stronger. They had a better understanding of what it took to win in the SEC. Freeze and his coaches had twice as much experience together in the league.

Almost anyone connected with Ole Miss would tell you it was worth getting beat a combined 58-14 by Alabama the previous two seasons to get this matchup played at Vaught-Hemingway.

It was sure to be a much tougher atmosphere than Nick Saban experienced in Oxford with LSU in 2003.

. . .

Two and a half hours before kickoff, Ole Miss was trending on Twitter. Katy Perry's appearance on *GameDay* was a marketing home run for the University and its football program.

Even before her arrival on the set for the show's final 15 minutes, the *GameDay* cast seemed giddy to finally be broadcasting from The Grove.

Fowler wore a tuxedo. Herbstreit said he was "honored" to be there.

GameDay senior producer, Lee Fitting, said at a Friday press conference that The Grove had been on the show's bucket list for a while.

"Behind closed doors in our little group, we talk about The Grove all the time. 'When are we going to get there? When is it going to fall on the right week? I want to get down there and I want to experience it,'" Fitting said. "Our crew typically after the show, most weeks, will leave and go home. "This week, there is a huge pack of us sticking around, tailgating in The Grove, going to the game, hanging out after the game. This is a big deal for us. This is a chance to introduce and explain to the country in further detail what The Grove is about."

But this *GameDay* will forever be remembered as Katy Perry's show. She wore a pink and black shag sweater and a plaid "school girl" skirt.

She correctly picked seven of nine games, including Notre Dame to beat Stanford because of the Irish's gold helmets and Tennessee to defeat Florida because it's what Dolly Parton would have done.

Perry also picked Auburn over LSU.

"Did you say LSU or LS-P.U.?" she asked Fowler, who gave her a look of good-natured disbelief.

Then she held up a corndog in her left hand and stared wide-eyed at the camera, a classic jab at the Bayou Bengals, one of Ole Miss' oldest and most despised rivals. LSU and corndogs became synonymous several years ago when an Auburn fan posted on the Rivals website that Tiger fans "smell like corndogs."

The Grove crowd cheered hysterically as Perry reached behind her and brought out an entire plate of corndogs. She yelled: "Hey, LSU! I heard you were hungry!"

When it came time to pick the Ole Miss-Alabama game, Howard went first: "I think the biggest difference in this game is going to be the quarterback play. I don't know if I trust Bo Wallace. Blake Sims, big game on the road in the SEC, but I still think Bo Wallace turns the ball over. I have Alabama in a close one."

Herbstreit seemed almost embarrassed to pick Alabama while seated in The Grove. But he did so, holding his left thumb and forefinger barely apart.

"Very, very close," he said.

When it was Perry's turn, she screamed the first line of Ole Miss' signature "Hotty Toddy" cheer: *"Are you ready?!?!?"* The fans finished it for her. Then came Corso's weekly moment of glory when he makes his pick by donning the head of the team's mascot, or raises some similar object related to the team. For the USC Trojans, for instance, he wielded the sword of the rider of the school's longtime mascot, a white horse named Traveler.

"Listen, I've been at ESPN for 27 years, and I've always wanted to come to this place, The Grove," Corso said. "It's the most beautiful place I've ever been. Beautiful girls, great campus, everything else. And I want The Grove to hear this pick. *Shhhhh!!!!!*"

He looked at Perry.

"Katy, you like music?" he asked.

"Ha! A bit."

"Let's hear this song then."

The sounds of the Lynyrd Skynyrd anthem, *Sweet Home Alabama,* played to a booing, thumbs-down crowd.

"Wait, wait. Cut the music," Corso said. "I couldn't do this to these great people ... "

He put on the head of Alabama's elephant mascot, Big Al.

"Noooooo!" said Perry, who began tossing corn dogs at the camera.

Corso shook Big Al's trunk in Perry's face a few times. Finally, she'd had enough. She grabbed the elephant head and threw it to the floor of the set. The fans answered with their loudest roar of the morning.

Afterward, she told ESPN's Samantha Ponder during an interview: "I didn't get a chance to go to college, but this is exactly what I dreamt it would be like. And I'm going to go out there [in The Grove] and drink some Bud Lite with everybody."

"Is the plan to hang out today?" Ponder asked.

"Oh, I'm going to watch the whole game," she said. "I think today is going to be a special day."

• • •

Bo watched *GameDay* from his room at the team's hotel in Tupelo, where the Rebels spent each Friday night before a home game.

He said Katy Perry was amusing and funny.

He said Desmond Howard's words — *"I'm not sure I trust Bo Wallace"* — were just noise. "After a while, you just learn to tune out that sort of stuff," he said. "Whatever Desmond Howard said would have no bearing on how I played. I was in control of that."

Chapter 23

Except for a 14 mile-per-hour northwest breeze, it was impossible for the weather to have been more glorious: Sunny and a high in the low 60s.

Moments before the 2:39 p.m. kickoff, Freeze reminded his players once more that they were talented enough to win.

"You've got a chance today to decide how much you value your standing right now in the college football world, and decide how much you want to fight for it today," Freeze told them. "It's time for you to crash the party. Crash ... this ... party."

Freeze then made, perhaps, his most fearless statement to that point as the Ole Miss head coach: "When this thing is over, and they start to tear the goal posts down ... them things are heavy so you better get back in here and don't get hurt, okay?"

• • •

In the TV booth, analyst Gary Danielson made his own bold statement on the air when partner Verne Lundquist asked him if the Rebels were "up to the task."

"I think they are," he said matter-of-factly, surely causing a collective soaring of blood pressure in the state next door.

He placed the possibility for an upset on Bo's shoulders.

"When teams beat Alabama, good quarterback play is one of the main reasons," Danielson said.

· · ·

Ole Miss won the coin toss and didn't play it safe by deferring until the second half. Freeze wanted the football.

College football's unpredictable nature was never more apparent than on the opening kickoff.

In their first four games, the Rebels had returned just five kickoffs for an average of six yards. Their chances were so few because opponents had only managed two touchdowns and six field goals. The preview "experts" listed the kickoff return game as a weakness.

Sophomore running back Mark Dodson didn't see it that way. He gathered the low, line-drive kick at the 7-yard line, cut right, weaved through traffic, received a key block from Channing Ward and hit an opening at the 30. He raced down the right sideline before stepping out of bounds at the Alabama 39.

Dodson's 54-yard return gave Ole Miss momentum and good field position just nine seconds into the game.

"It's time for me to start throwing my body around ... "

Bo fulfilled that night-before promise on the game's first play, a designed quarterback draw that he ran up the middle for 10 yards and a first down.

The next three plays netted zero. Freeze sent out true freshman kicker Gary Wunderlich, whose last field goal attempt had been in high school. From 46 yards, with Will Denny snapping and Ryan Buchanan holding, he kicked it long and high and true to give the Rebels a 3-0 lead.

Bo greeted his offensive linemen as they trotted off the field with fist bumps and pats on the helmet.

Alabama's Adam Griffith missed a 46-yard field goal on the Tide's first possession. Bo ran another quarterback draw for 15 yards on the ensuing drive. He also passed 10 yards to Mathers and 12 yards to Core. But Freeze called on Fletcher — not Wunderlich — for a 33-yard field goal try with 3:47 left in the first quarter. It sailed wide right.

The defenses turned the game into a prizefight and a punting match. Alabama's lanky 6-foot-5 true freshman, JK Scott, boomed punts of 57 and 49 yards, and kicked another 33 yards to pin the Rebels at their 18. Will Gleeson answered with punts of 50 and 47 yards. Wunderlich also punted one 40 yards.

On the second play of the second quarter, Alabama lost one of its top weapons, running back Kenyan Drake, to a gruesome injury.

Drake caught a quick pass and darted left and up the field. He was sandwiched by Tony Conner and Bryon Bennett at the Ole Miss 39. When the play ended, Drake's left foot and ankle were pointed in a different direction than the rest of his leg. He screamed with pain. Senquez Golson saw it and sprinted away in horror. Conner and Robert Nkemdiche also ran toward the Ole Miss sideline with their hands on top of their helmets. Drake was done for the season.

With seven minutes left in the first half, Alabama's offense put together a drive. Running back T.J. Yeldon gained 45 yards on nine carries, and Sims completed three passes for 29 yards.

Alabama faced fourth-and-goal at the Ole Miss 1-yard line. Sims faked to Yeldon off right tackle. The defense bit, and Sims easily bootlegged left into the end zone. Alabama led 7-3 with 3:27 left until halftime.

Wommack's first-team defense had finally surrendered a touchdown, 10 quarters into the season.

Again, the teams swapped punts: Gleeson 55 yards and into the end zone; Scott 64 yards to the Ole Miss 18 with 51 seconds left.

Freeze was pleased with how things had gone in the first half. "I thought we had some things [on offense] that we could hit them with in the second half," he said.

Content to be down just 7-3 at intermission and 82 yards from the end zone, Freeze decided to run out the half. But first, he and Werner wanted to see how Alabama aligned its defense against a particular formation. One innocent running play and then head to the dressing room.

Bo handed the ball to Mathers going straight ahead, but penetration by the Alabama defense forced him wide left. Tide cornerback Cyrus Jones came up to tackle Mathers at the 15 but grabbed and turned his facemask. As Mathers' head turned, so did his shoulders and his left arm, exposing the football. Jones swatted it out of Mathers' grasp, scooped it up inches from the sideline and tight-roped 8 yards into the end zone for a touchdown.

The facemask wasn't called. Alabama suddenly led 14-3.

"A catastrophic mistake by the official," Danielson said on the broadcast.

Nick Saban, who usually appears miserable on the sidelines no matter the score, wore a wide smile as he greeted Jones with a pat on the helmet and the rump.

Following the ensuing kickoff, Ole Miss ran out the clock.

"Bo Wallace, still no touchdowns in his career against Alabama, halfway through this one," CBS studio host Adam Zucker pointed out.

• • •

There was no yelling or pointing fingers, no throwing of objects inside the Ole Miss locker room at halftime.

"Nobody was freaking out," Bo said. "I could hear the defense on the other side of the room saying 'We've got to get our offense the ball back.' On a lot of teams, the defense would have been saying 'Can you believe we'd held them to one touchdown and the offense goes and gives them a freebie?' That's not us, though. That's not this team."

Freeze was understandably shaken and frustrated during his interview with Allie LeForce leaving the field at the end of the half.

Players have an innate ability to detect fear or doubt in opponents. They also can sense it among teammates and coaches.

In Freeze's case, it had never been difficult to demand the players "play the next play" and "do not blink when something bad happens" during mid-week team meetings or games against middle-of-the-road competition.

But what about when trailing by 11 to the No. 1-ranked team in the country because of a fluke play and an obvious blown call by an official?

Freeze practiced what he preached. He stood before his players with belief and conviction.

"You belong in this game," he told them. "You're good enough to win it, and you never blink. Do … not … "

"Blink!" players finished his sentence.

"Tempo, offense. Time to pick it up," Freeze said. "Let's go. 'All in' on three. One, two … "

"All in!"

• • •

In the first 10 plays of the third quarter, Alabama moved from its 20 to the Ole Miss 24 and had a first-and 10.

But Sims lost 6 yards on a fake and keep left, Rebel defenders Serderius Bryant, Cody Prewitt and Mike Hilton swarming him. After an incomplete pass, Bennett and Bryant forced Sims to scramble out of bounds on third down for a 4-yard loss.

The two negative plays turned a 41-yard field goal attempt into a 51-yarder. Griffith, who was silently battling a stress fracture in his back, shanked it badly to the left.

Griffith had faced tougher times. When he was 13, his name was Andrzej Dombowksi and his home was an orphanage in Poland. His father had just been released from prison. He spoke no English, but that didn't stop a couple from Calhoun, Georgia from making Dombowski the only teenager adopted out of Poland in 2006. His biological father told him it was a good opportunity for a better life. Dombowski took on the Georgia couple's last name. He chose to be known as Adam because it was short and easy to spell.

It was eight years ago to the day that he left Poland for Georgia.

• • •

"I've never seen a team like this. Of course, we haven't had any adversity yet ... How are we going to react? I think I know how, but you never really know until you go through it. At some point we'll find out." — Bo Wallace, one day after the Rebels defeated Vanderbilt in the second week of the season.

Ole Miss had reached that point, especially the offense.

Freeze wasted no time in going to one of those "things" he thought could hurt Alabama. On second-and-12 from the 32, Ole Miss hurried and lined up in a trips formation right, the short side of the field.

Part of the Rebels' game plan was to force Alabama senior inside linebacker Trey DePriest to turn and run in pass coverage with Evan Engram or Jaylen Walton.

They got the coverage they wanted. Engram, the inside receiver in the trips alignment, ran straight up the field between the numbers and the hash marks, splitting the corner and the safety. DePriest took one step forward, and Engram blew past him. Bo threw a dart that Engram caught at the Alabama 42 and ran to the 18 for a gain of 50 yards.

Bo ran off right tackle for 4 yards, continuing the offense's commitment to run-throw balance. Then on second down, Bo looked to his right as the teams lined up. Freshman cornerback Tony Brown was one-on-one with Treadwell — a young 6-foot defender on a seasoned 6-foot-3 receiver.

Bo delivered a perfect back-shoulder throw to Treadwell before he ever turned around. He caught it at the 5, broke free of Brown, cut inside safety Nick Perry and ran into the end zone with a 14-yard touchdown reception.

"Alabama is going to play us man ... if they do, I think we can beat them. We have better athletes outside than they do." — Bo the night before.

In four plays and a little more than a minute, Ole Miss' offense delivered a touchdown and a statement: It wasn't going to fold because of one bad break. Not this team. Not this day.

Alabama's lead was 14-10 with 7:20 left in the third quarter.

On the ensuing kickoff, Ole Miss' Marquis Haynes knocked a blocker into Alabama return man Christion Jones, who then cut left and had the ball punched loose by Channing Ward at the Tide 14. Jones was somehow able to recover it, but it was clear the Ole Miss coverage team was playing with an edge.

It was also clear Alabama would not wilt. On the third play of the next possession, Sims passed 53 yards to his junior tight end, O.J. Howard, who was wide open down the right seam. Golson ran him down at the Ole Miss 19, and the Rebel defense forced the Tide to attempt another field goal. Griffin nailed this one from 44 yards with 3:54 left in the third quarter. Alabama 17, Ole Miss 10.

On the next to last play of the quarter, on third-and-5 at the Alabama 48, Bo tried to connect with Sanders on a skinny post to the right. But the pass was deflected by defensive lineman Jarran Reed and fell incomplete. Ole Miss would have to punt.

These are the moments when fans can only see a single result and not the entire picture.

Bo ran to the sideline and said to Freeze: "We got 'em, Coach. They can't cover us.' "

Freeze nodded.

"I knew we would hit some of those in the fourth quarter," Bo said.

Alabama began going to its money receiver. Two third-down passes to Amari Cooper gained 34 yards and two first downs. But the Tide eventually had to punt with 11:31 remaining.

On third-and-8 from the Ole Miss 22, the offensive line gave Bo protection. He was able to work to his fourth progression, a crossing route to Core for 14 yards.

Two plays later, on third-and-9, Bo made one of the best throws of his career — a thread-the-needle pass over a linebacker and between two defensive backs to slot receiver Markell Pack on a skinny post. It was a great play on both ends, Bo delivering the ball and knowing he was about to get smacked by linebacker Ryan Anderson, who came free from Bo's left. Pack, a true freshman, snatched the ball out of the air as if he were a senior. First down at the Alabama 45.

"A gutsy throw by Bo Wallace right there," Danielson called it.

"I checked to that play at the line, and then I saw they were bringing more rushers than we could block. The play clock was down to like 4 seconds so I couldn't check out of it," Bo said. "[Anderson] got me good, but I actually don't even remember feeling the hit. And I never saw Markell catch it. I just hoped to hear the crowd yell. That's how I knew he had."

Jordan Wilkins ran for no gain, and on second-and-10 with 8:45 left Ole Miss ran a four-receiver bunch set to the right. Engram ran a post — right past safety Landon Collins. Bo put it in Engram's hands at the 22 on what looked to be a game-tying touchdown. But the steady sophomore dropped it.

Bo showed no emotion. Hands on his hips and watching a replay on the Jumbotron on the north end of the stadium. Then he looked to the sidelines to get the next play.

An incomplete pass to Treadwell forced another punt, and Gleeson again did his part, placing the ball out at the 1-yard line.

The defense forced a second consecutive three-and-out, and Scott boomed another punt, 60 yards. Pack returned it 9 yards to the Ole Miss 44 with 6:24 left.

Walton ran left for 6 yards on first down. Bo hit Engram for 16 yards on a corner route left to the Alabama 34.

"We had seen on film that play would work," Bo said. "We made them roll a safety [to the defense's left] by motioning Laquon that way. That left the corner route on the other side wide open."

Freeze and Werner went to a trips right formation on the next play. Sanders, the outside receiver, split the corner and safety on a post pattern. The line gave Bo time once again, and he connected with Sanders for a 34-yard touchdown pass. Wunderlich's extra point tied the game 17-17 with

5:29 left.

"Once again," Danielson said, "it's not Bad Bo, not Good Bo. It was Great Bo."

"I was watching Landon Collins the whole way," Bo said. "As soon as he took one step down, I knew I had Vince. He really broke down that corner [Brown] with a great move, and then ran an absolutely perfect route. Like I've said all along, Vince is great. He deserves more credit than he gets."

The offensive line on that game-tying drive, left to right: Tunsil, Morris, Still, Bell, and Cooper.

Denzel Nkemdiche greeted Bo when he reached the sideline.

"That throw was for all them people that have hated on you for three years!" Denzel screamed above a deafening crowd.

Bo responded: "I ain't through yet. We're about to win this game."

• • •

On the touchdown, Engram was flagged for unsportsmanlike conduct for taking off his helmet while still on the field. So Wunderlich would kick off from the 20 instead of the 35. Alabama seemed certain to gain good field position.

But special teams coach Tom Allen has preached his own messages to the kickoff coverage team all season: Hit them in the mouth. Find a way to win the game. Light somebody up.

"Provide the winning edge" — the special teams' "it" factor.

Christion Jones fielded the kickoff near the right sideline at the 12, ran diagonally to the 32 where Channing Ward once again stripped him of the football. This time, Ole Miss' Kailo Moore recovered at the 31.

On first down, Walton ran right, cut past an arm tackle in the backfield and was met by Alabama junior defensive back Maurice Smith at the 27. Walton overpowered Smith for another 5 yards — 166 pounds whipping

199 pounds with the game on the line for a gain of 9.

"That run right there showed our mindset and our will to win that game," Bo said.

For years, Alabama had always been the strongest team in the fourth quarter. One of Freeze's most important hires after taking the job was strength and conditioning coach Paul Jackson. His workout program was paying off. So was the financial commitment Bjork had made to increasing the strength and conditioning staff.

Freeze called another running play on second-and-1.

"Alabama brought both safeties up, and I saw [Brown] one on one with Laquon again," Bo said. "I gave Laquon a little signal. Everybody else on the offense thought it was a run except me and him."

Another back-shoulder throw to Treadwell gained 12 yards and a first down at the Alabama 10.

Morris tweaked his knee during the play. Bell moved to left guard and Rod Taylor stepped in at right guard. Walton gained 2 on first down.

Freeze made a curious call on second down, replacing Bo with the 295-pound Liggins as a "wildcat" quarterback.

"I thought we might try to pound it in. So I wasn't upset about coming out," Bo said.

Instead, Liggins faked to Wilkins left, and rolled right looking to throw. He was met by three Alabama defenders as he carried the ball with one hand. Somehow, he held on but was dropped for 2-yard loss.

"I saw him bootleg it and waving the ball around … that's the only time I freaked out all day," Bo said.

Freeze let the clock run to 2:59 left and called a timeout. Bo again went to his linemen and gave them a fist bump.

This was the biggest play call in Freeze's two-plus years at Ole Miss: Third and 8 at the Alabama 10 in a tie game.

Ole Miss wasted no time lining up and snapping the ball. Flexed out about 5 yards right, Engram ran a slant that occupied a linebacker. Landon Collins also took a couple of steps toward Engram. Treadwell turned at the line of scrimmage as if it was going to be a quick pass, causing the cornerback to run up.

What those two patterns did was open a crease for Walton to run a quick wheel route to the end zone. Collins saw it and closed fast, but Walton was past him. Bo threw it over Collins' head and into the chest of Walton, who caught it, tapped both feet down in the end zone even though one would have been aplenty. Touchdown. Ole Miss grabbed a 23-17 lead with 2:54 left.

Bo received a flying chest bump from graduate assistant coach Robert Ratliff just before reaching the sideline.

"All I could think about was 'We just beat them,' " he said. "It felt so great because of all the bullshit I'd taken from that fan base over there. I saw them crying in the stands, freaking out, not knowing what to think or how to act. I looked at them in the north end zone when the touchdown was being reviewed and I thought, 'This is awesome.' "

But the drama was far from over.

• • •

Ole Miss blew the extra point. Twice. Wunderlich banged an attempt off the left upright, but Alabama's Tony Brown was flagged for roughing the kicker. Freeze switched to Fletcher for the second try, and his kick was blocked by Brown.

Alabama could take the lead with a touchdown and an extra point.

"I was thinking 'no way this is happening to us,' " Bo said.

Alabama got the ball at its 13-yard line with 2:44 remaining after a 20-yard return by Cyrus Jones and a block-in-the-back penalty on the Tide.

Ole Miss' defense had yielded one touchdown all day, three touchdowns all season. Alabama had to move 87 yards with only one timeout.

The yards came at a steady clip: Sims scrambled for 3. Sims passed to Christion Jones for 17. Yeldon rushed for 8. Sims passed to Cooper for 30. Sims passed to Yeldon for 7.

With the clock inside a minute left, Alabama had moved to the Ole Miss 22 where it faced second and 3. Sims again scrambled, this time for 4 yards and a first down. But Howard was penalized for holding Marquis Haynes as Sims ran past him.

Second and 13 at the 32 with 44 seconds left. Alabama decided to go for it all.

Howard ran a seam route between the right hash and the numbers, and Sims lofted a beautiful throw to the end zone. Howard had a step on Prewitt and appeared to be open, but Golson came over the top of the play from his left corner position. Howard ran past the goal line with his arms outstretched, awaiting to cradle the football. He never saw the 5-foot-9, 176-pound Golson, who out-jumped the 6-foot-6, 242-pound Howard for the ball.

Incomplete, the official ruled, motioning that Golson came down out of the end zone.

"I knew I had it," Golson said postgame. "When I caught it and came down, I saw my left foot hit the blue [end zone turf] and I knew I had caught it cleanly."

The play went to an official review.

Ole Miss cheered when a replay on the jumbotron showed Golson's left foot touch down in bounds.

Secondary coach Jason Jones was giving his unit instructions in case Alabama retained the football, but Golson's eyes were locked on veteran referee Matt Loeffler as he walked onto the field to deliver the replay ruling.

"After further review, the ball was intercepted in the end zone ... "

Ole Miss fans roared. Linebacker Christian Russell grabbed Golson from behind and lifted him off the ground. Saban, who had turned his back as Loeffler announced the ruling, took off his headset.

Two snaps, two kneel downs and the game would be over.

"We practice it every Friday," Bo said. "We call it 'victory.' I told the center to snap it on 'first sound.' The linemen were telling each other, 'Nobody touches Bo!' I remember Jaylen yelling that at them, too."

Bo took the first snap, and flipped the ball to Loeffler. He noticed fans starting to run onto the field and he calmly motioned "stop" with his hands. In the TV booth, Danielson said: "Forever more, Bo Wallace will be able to come to The Grove and tell the story about how he quarterbacked the upset of the No. 1 team, Alabama."

Bo took the snap, knelt and flipped the ball to Loeffler again. But this time he asked for it back. He tucked it under his right arm, and as Ole Miss fans stormed onto the field, Bo weaved his way down the right sideline, to Section A, Row 1 where his family sat for every home game. He tossed the ball to Bryce.

Fans were still pouring out of the stands to celebrate together and with their team. And, yes, to tear down the goal post in the South end zone, as Freeze told his team they would.

For a split second, Bo almost ran into the locker room to avoid the madness.

"But it hit me, 'My time is getting short here.' So I went back out to celebrate, too," he said.

Fans were taking selfies with him, patting his shoulder pads, tapping his helmet.

Suddenly, a male cheerleader and a fan scooped him up and onto their shoulders. Others helped hold him aloft. He was paraded through the people, sharing high-fives all around.

At one point, someone reached out a hand and touched the back of Bo's jersey. The hand stayed there for a few seconds. Then the person shook his head and smiled up at Bo, who smiled back.

It was Laquon Treadwell, who was happy to see his friend rewarded in such a heroic and memorable way.

"That was my favorite moment, Quon smiling at me," Bo said. "Being carried off was awesome. A lot of things flashed through my mind ... all the criticism I'd taken, the 'Good Bo, Bad Bo' thing. And I couldn't help but think, 'These people who are carrying me off and loving on me ... some of them are the same people who booed me when the starting lineups were announced before the Texas A&M game my sophomore year. And the next time I screw up, they'll probably boo me again.' "

Danielson offered a final thought as the cameras showed fans continuing to flood the field: "We talked about at halftime that Ole Miss needed some offense. They had 105 yards. Well, they put 218 yards on Alabama, the most Alabama has given up in the second half in two years."

Bo started making his way toward the dressing room, hugging and high-fiving as he walked. A young man, smiling and screaming, ran up to Bo, grabbed his arms and shook a head full of brown hair on the front of Bo's jersey.

The field was covered with fans three-quarters of the way toward the north end zone. Indeed, the goal post came down and was carried on the shoulders of students into Sunday's wee hours all over campus and Oxford's town square.

"Wait and see. October 4th, we will beat Alabama."

Seventy-three days earlier, Bo had said it would happen. I reminded him of that postgame and he smiled. "I'm not gonna tell you wrong," he said and laughed.

"You had tears in your eyes coming out of the dressing room before the game," I told him.

"Naw," he said.

"Yes, you did. That's the most emotional I've ever seen you."

"Naw, man, No way," he said.

"I know what I saw."

He changed the subject.

It was one of the greatest victories in school history, the first win ever by the Rebels over a No. 1-ranked opponent, a giant statement to the rest of the SEC — and a reminder to their fan base.

"You give us a chance, we're going to win you over, we're going to win recruits and

we're going to win football games."

Freeze's promise on the day he was hired carried more weight than ever. Ole Miss was 5-0 for the first time in 52 years.

And Vaught-Hemingway Stadium, which had absorbed more than its share of heartache, was treated to a soothing bath of joyous tears as the old battleground got a jump on its 100th birthday celebration that would come in 2015.

• • •

One could say this victory was for a lot of Rebels who suffered heartache at the hands of Alabama.

For the 1969 team, led by Archie Manning, that lost 33-32 at Birmingham's Legion Field in one of the first college football games broadcast in prime time.

For the 1993 team, which featured one of Ole Miss' most talented defensive teams but couldn't tackle a 5-foot-7, 172-pound water bug named David Palmer, who accounted for 168 of the Tide's 279 yards of total offense. The Rebels lost to the fourth-ranked Tide 19-14 in Oxford, allowing four field goals and one touchdown set up by a 54-yard pass by Palmer.

And for the 2007 team, which surrendered a 7-point lead in the final seven minutes and lost 27-24, and for the co-ed who was so furious at a replay official, she tossed her red high heels onto the field. Ole Miss rallied and seemed to be set for a shot at a game-winning play — or at least a tying field goal — when Seth Adams threw 41 yards to Shay Hodge to the Alabama 4-yard line with 7 seconds left. The replay official over turned the play, saying Hodge stepped out of bounds on his own before making the catch. Hodge and Ole Miss argued he was forced out of bounds by a defensive back.

But in 2014, it was the Rebels' turn to dish out the hurt. Afterward, Ole Miss was one of 12 undefeated FBS teams remaining.

"I felt confident all year, really," Freeze said postgame. "I felt like we had defensive depth. When you play good defense, you have a chance. Our special teams have been solid. I see the accountability growing on our team.

"This week, I've enjoyed the heck out of it. I've enjoyed the preparation. Our time was stressed a little bit, but I was really confident. I like the way our kids go about preparing for games. We don't get too emotional or too dejected."

And the Rebels have playmakers.

Golson's interception in the final minute was his SEC-best fourth of the season. He earned it by learning from a previous mistake.

"Earlier in the game, I had blown that coverage," Golson said, referring to Howard's 53-yard catch in the third quarter. "We were in Cover 3 and they hit the tight end up the [seam], which was my fault. They ran the same exact play again. I just did my job, was in the right spot and made a good play."

Bo completed 18 of 31 passes for 251 yards and three touchdowns, no interceptions. In the fourth quarter, he completed 6 of 9 throws for 105 yards and two touchdowns.

As soon as Bo walked into the locker room and took off his pads, Freeze approached him. The two embraced and shared a few words. An Ole Miss photographer captured the moment.

"He said, 'I'm so happy for you. You deserved this, and the fans will never forget this day,'" Bo recalled. "I appreciated it. I was happy for him, too. But I think that was the first time he ever said in so many words, 'Thank you' to me. I'll never forget it."

"It's one of my favorite pictures," Freeze said. "Knowing full well what the public's perspective was of his and my journey together, and knowing what he started as — a young man who was somewhat irresponsible and maybe not totally buying in as a quarterback. Seeing all that and then seeing him grow to what he had become his senior year, to see him getting the reward of beating the gold standard in our sport, and knowing that all of the naysayers will eventually fade away but that Alabama victory won't … it was a special moment in our journey together."

At the postgame press conference, Freeze said when asked about Bo's performance: "Sometimes these kids take way more criticism than they deserve. I don't know that they get the equal treatment on the other side of it. Bo managed the game extremely well for us. We really felt like our defense was good enough to keep us in it against a very, very talented offense that stresses you in all kinds of ways. He managed the game very nicely.

"In the second half, he made some big-time plays. He just played so solid. On that last touchdown, that ball was right where it needed to be for us. Who knows what the next week holds? But tonight Bo led his team to defeat the No. 1 team in the country. He deserves credit for being a big part of that."

Trina Wallace saw none of the game.

"I couldn't watch," she said. "I had my head buried in my hands, and people were telling me what happened after the play. It's just so much pressure on Bo, and I don't want him to mess up and have people come down on him."

She's heard it on countless occasions.

"I was walking from our tent in The Grove after one game and these people in front of me were talking about what a dumb ass quarterback he was," Trina said. "I try to bite my tongue, but I finally said, 'Excuse me, but that *dumb ass* you're talking about happens to be my son!' Their eyes got real big and I let them have it pretty good.

"I'm so happy for him to be able to be on the team that beat Alabama. And I can't wait to watch the game when I get home. We record them all."

Trina got the one thing she had hoped for after the game — a family photo outside the Manning Center.

Usually, they were able to visit with Bo for a few minutes after games, but not always. Especially after night games in Oxford, they would immediately head back to Pulaski, 190 miles away, where Bill has worked for 25 years at a steel plant. He has volunteered for the Sunday shift, which begins at 5 a.m., so he can make overtime pay to help fund their trips to every game.

. . .

Bo hadn't gone out much, if at all, the entire season. Not even after games. The risks far outweighed the rewards.

"But I had a lot of friends in town from back home, and we all went out," he said. "It was the best night I've had since I've been at Ole Miss. And it wasn't just about me. I loved seeing how happy all my teammates were and the Ole Miss fans were. That's what makes it so special, when you can help deliver something like that to them."

He seemed his even-keeled self after the game. But after going to get a quick breakfast Sunday morning around 10, he sat in his car when he returned to his apartment.

The emotions poured out of him.

"It was like it finally hit me," he said. "The magnitude of the win, how things seemed to be turning around for the program — and for me. We were going to move way up in the rankings, and people were finally saying, 'Well, maybe Bo *can* play some football.' To have things go 180 degrees from they way it had been at times the first two years ... I took that time to myself. And I'm glad I did."

Bo, after the Alabama game, carried on the shoulders of fans

Chapter 24

The Associated Press' Top 25 poll on Sunday had the nation — and Mississippians — having to look twice to believe it.

Ole Miss and Mississippi State were tied at No. 3, ahead of programs such as Notre Dame, Michigan State, Oregon, Georgia, and Ohio State. Both were 5-0 overall, 2-0 in the SEC. It was the first time in history the two programs were in the Top 10 at the same time.

Florida State held on at No. 1, and Alabama fell to No. 7.

Suddenly, Ole Miss and Mississippi State were the darlings of the national media. *Sports Illustrated* featured both teams on the cover under a headline that read "Mississippi Mayhem" and devoted an 11-page spread to the teams' landscape-changing victories (State defeated Texas A&M 48-31 in Starkville). The first line of the subhead on the Ole Miss story read: "You'll remember the first weekend in October as the moment Hotty Toddy went national, like Roll Tide or War Eagle."

"They're deserving," Freeze said of State. "I think we're deserving. Will we be deserving three weeks from now? Who knows? Saturday was a great day for the state of Mississippi for sure."

Indeed, the Rebels and the Bulldogs were walking among the elite. But both had their hands full on the Saturday ahead. State would play No. 2 Auburn in Starkville, while Ole Miss was in College Station to face an angry and embarrassed A&M team.

Even before the season, many figured this would be a difficult game for

Ole Miss, win or lose against Alabama. The Rebels needed to recharge their emotions, and A&M couldn't afford another loss in the SEC West.

Because part of Kyle Field's renovation and expansion was completed, Freeze's team most likely would be playing before the largest football crowd ever assembled in the state of Texas — approximately 109,000.

Those on the outside saw roadblocks to reaching 6-0. Ole Miss' coaches and players saw nothing but a giant opportunity.

"If we don't beat A&M, the Alabama game won't mean nearly as much," Bo said. "I think the coaches will rely a lot on the seniors and the older guys to keep people focused."

• • •

On Monday morning, Bo learned he had been named the SEC Offensive Player of the Week. The press release from the league office noted that Bo ranked second in the SEC in passing yards per game (304.4) and touchdown passes (14.) It also mentioned he had started all 31 games since joining the team.

• • •

After he exited a quarterbacks meeting Thursday afternoon before practice, Bo went to his locker and checked his cell.

"I had all kind of notifications on my phone," he said. "The week of a game, I usually have a good many. But I probably had 40 to 50 when I looked. I was like 'What the heck could be going on?'"

A rumor was spreading on Twitter that Bo had been arrested Wednesday night in Oxford.

I was certain it wasn't true. We had talked for more than an hour that night. Right before we hung up, he mentioned how excited he was the season was unfolding the way it had, and that the leaders were emphasizing to the younger players the importance of "protecting the team by not doing anything stupid."

Bo quickly sent out his own tweet. He took a selfie in the locker room and included this message:

lol getting ready for practice Def didn't get arrested last night C'mon Twitter Get real

Bo asked Kyle Campbell at practice if they had any idea who had started the rumor. "He said they thought it was a fan from another team who had a fake Twitter account," Bo said.

"It's all part of being an SEC quarterback," Bo said. "You need skills to be able to play the position in this league, but you'd better be mentally tough, too. If you're not, you won't last long in the SEC."

• • •

The night before the game, Bo talked about the difference in this year's A&M team compared to the last two.

"Well, we don't have to worry about Johnny Manziel running out and winning the game in the last couple of minutes," Bo said. "I haven't seen anybody like him in college football. Ever. He did things that nobody else can do."

Freeze reminded the media of that during his segment on the mid-week SEC tele-conference. He talked about Manziel helping deliver two of the most heartbreaking losses of the Freeze era.

In 2012, Ole Miss led 27-17 midway of the third quarter and had A&M pinned at its 3-yard line on third-and-19. Manziel, on his way to winning the Heisman Trophy as a redshirt freshman, passed 32 yards to wideout Mike Evans, who made a leaping grab over a Rebel defender. Two plays later, Manziel ran 29 yards for a touchdown.

With just over three minutes left, Freeze decided to go for it on fourth-and-1 at the Ole Miss 39. He believed the Rebels had a better chance of gaining one yard than stopping Manziel on a late drive — and that was no disrespect to his defensive squad.

But running back Jeff Scott was stuffed for no gain on a give off left tackle. With 1:46 left, Manziel threw 20 yards to Ryan Swoope in the end zone for the game-winner. It ended when Bo was intercepted at the A&M 32 with a minute remaining.

In 2013, the wacky SEC schedule brought A&M back to Oxford. Same song, same verse.

Bo put Ole Miss ahead, 38-31, on a 50-yard touchdown pass to Jaylen Walton with 6:05 left. But Maziel ran 6 yards for a touchdown to tie it, then led the Aggies in position for a 33-yard field goal as time expired.

Ole Miss could take comfort that Manziel had moved on to the NFL's Cleveland Browns — the 22nd player taken in the 2014 draft — but the Aggies' defense was improved and leading the league in sacks with 19.

"What concerns me," Bo said, "is that it's going to be really loud at A&M and some of our linemen — Fahn Cooper, Ben Still — haven't been in a place like that before. We need to get off to a fast start, and the line just has to stay composed and be confident.

"It's going to be a long day tomorrow, sitting around the hotel and waiting for an 8 o'clock kickoff. I wish we could play the game right now."

• • •

Triple-decked Kyle Field was packed with 110,633 fans. It sounded like three times that many as game time approached.

Again, Freeze came up with just the right message in the dressing room moments before kickoff: "There are about 110,000 of them out there, and about 120 of us. And you know what? I like those odds."

ESPN's No. 1 announcing team was in the booth, Chris Fowler and Kirk Herbstreit — fresh off their *GameDay* visit to The Grove.

After three-and-outs by both teams, Ole Miss cruised 69 yards in 5 plays to take a 7-0 lead. Bo threw to Core for 13, to Treadwell for 21, to Adeboyejo

— once an A&M commitment — for 31 to the Aggie 4-yard line. Bo ran it in for a touchdown on a keep right for 4 yards. Wunderlich, who was named the No. 1 kicker by Freeze during the week, made the point-after.

"Quincy would've scored if he hadn't cut back left," Bo said. "I told him on the sideline, 'Hey, if you want to cut back, I'll take that rushing touchdown.' He laughed. After we watched film Sunday, he told me 'I have no idea what I was thinking there.'"

Bo had no idea what A&M was thinking.

"I had asked the coaches to go-four wide and run verticals, which we did," Bo said. "I looked pre-snap, and I had Quincy with nobody over the top. I remember back in spring practice getting the same look against our defense — they had a nickel back on Quincy with nobody over the top. I turned to Coach Freeze that day and asked, 'Why would a defense do that? Quincy will run right by them.' It worked that day and it worked again in the A&M game."

Bo's 10-yard rushing touchdown capped a 99-yard drive — Ole Miss' first since 1989 — the next time the Rebels had the ball to make it 14-0. Passes to Engram for 18, Treadwell for 11 and Core for 18 — plus 25 yards rushing by Walton — set up the score.

Both touchdowns came on the same play call. "It's part of our tempo package, and we had noticed A&M was slow lining up when teams got closer to the end zone."

On the first series of the second quarter, Prewitt intercepted Kenny Hill's pass and returned it 75 yards for a touchdown.

With 11:56 left in the first half, Ole Miss led 21-0. A&M's fans had been shocked into silence.

"Did you notice our bench after Cody scored on the interception?" Bo asked. "We were happy about it. We high-fived. But we weren't just going crazy. We've come to expect to be ahead, and we've come to expect plays like that. I think that says so much about where our team is right now."

At halftime, Ole Miss had outgained A&M 225 to 174 overall, but 97-28 on the ground — meaning the Rebels were whipping the Aggies at the line of scrimmage. It was the first time since Sumlin came to A&M in 2012 that his offense had been shut out in the first two quarters.

Freeze hammered home one message at halftime: *Finish*.

A&M pulled to within 21-7 with 7:05 left in the third quarter with a 14-play, 58-yard drive.

But Bo's 33-yard touchdown pass to Adeboyejo with 13 seconds left in the third quarter stretched the lead to 28-7.

On the nine play, 65-yard drive, Bo made a play the folks in Giles County had seen before — and it was an important one. Trying to answer the Aggies' touchdown, the Rebels faced third-and 8 at their 37. Bo looked to throw, took off up the middle, then cut right. Two A&M defenders were between him and the first down. So, he did exactly what he had in the high school playoffs — he went airborne. He took off between the 42- and 43-yard line, went up and over the defenders, and stretched the ball as far as he could.

First down at the 46. It immediately became known as Superman II in Pulaksi.

Herbstreit said: "That's a senior who is tired of hearing about how erratic he can be."

It may have been the most important play of the game. With A&M hanging within two touchdowns, Ole Miss extended its lead six plays after the leap. Bo connected with Adeboyejo for 33 yards and a touchdown. Ole Miss led 28-7 with 13 seconds left in the third quarter.

A 21-yard fumble return for a touchdown on the second play of the fourth quarter for a touchdown by senior linebacker Keith Lewis — one of the Rebels' most underrated players —made it 35-7.

A&M scored on two pass plays in the final 8:47, one of them on the game's final play.

Final score: Ole Miss 35, A&M 20. The Rebels improved to 6-0, 3-0 in the SEC. The whipping was physical and thorough.

Bo completed 13 of 19 passes for 178 yards and a touchdown, no interceptions. He also rushed 14 times for a team-high 50 yards. Walton ran

Bo diving over two Texas A&M defenders to gain a first down

for 49. Treadwell caught 5 passes for 53 yards.

Gleeson continued to be a force with 7 punts for an average of 42.7 and three kicks downed inside the 20-yard line.

But again, the Rebel defense was overpowering, limiting A&M to just 54 yards rushing and one score when the game had even a sliver of doubt left. It forced three turnovers and now led the SEC with 13. Wommack's Landsharks grabbed two more interceptions, giving them a nation's best 12. Three had been returned for touchdowns. And freshman end Marquis Haynes had both Rebel sacks, giving him 4 for the season.

• • •

When it was 21-0 late in the second half, Bo looked at some of his teammates. They had the same expression on their faces that he did.

"We were all thinking, 'I knew we were good, but we may be the best team in the country,'" Bo said. "I even told Laquon after the game, 'There isn't a team out there better than we are.' We were playing better than anybody. The only team that could come close to matching our swagger at that moment was Mississippi State. They were playing good, too."

Freeze said he thought the same thing that night leaving College Station.

"Well, *one* of the best," the coach said. "We were playing awfully well. We just needed to keep everybody healthy."

Chapter 25

It was officially Tennessee Volunteers week, and Trina Wallace was having a hard time focusing at her job in Pulaski.

"I hope Ole Miss beats them 100-0," she said on the Monday before the game at Vaught-Hemingway Stadium. "It's nothing against Coach [Butch] Jones because he wasn't even the head coach when they didn't give Bo the time of day. And I'm still a Tennessee women's basketball fan. But it's hard to forget the fact that Tennessee never thought Bo was worth recruiting."

Bo had long looked forward to playing against Tennessee. But now that it was here, his focus had changed: It was more about winning and being impressive doing so, rather than who the opponent happened to be.

Especially since the new AP poll was out. Ole Miss remained No. 3, but Mississippi State jumped to No. 1 after beating Auburn 38-23, the Bulldogs' third straight victory over a Top 10-ranked team. Defending national champion Florida State slipped to No. 2.

Ole Miss received three first-place votes: Eric Hansen, *South Bend Tribune*; John Shinn, *Norman (Okla.) Transcript*; Chad Cripe of the *Idaho Statesman*.

"I'm not upset about State being No. 1," Bo said. "Let them have their time in the sun because it's all going to come to an end in about six weeks or so, anyway, when we play them — if not sooner. I'm thinking about Tennessee and nothing else."

Bo on the Walk of Champions before the Tennessee game

And with good reason. The Vols had split their first six games. Two of their losses were back-to-back heartbreakers at Georgia 35-32 and 10-9 against Florida.

Jones, who replaced Derek Dooley following the 2012 season, put together the No. 4 recruiting class of 2014, according to Scout. Twenty-one of those signees had already played.

"They're scary on tape," Freeze said of Tennessee. "They're playing very passionate football with great young talent. That's how we were after our first full recruiting class. We played a ton of freshmen just like they're doing. It's only a matter of time before they break through."

Bo said the coaches had told him "to chill out on running the football this week."

"I think they're just trying to save me from taking as many hits as they can," he said. "There is a chance DeVante might come in and run some. They've put a package together for him. But you never know how a game will go."

• • •

In front of the third-largest crowd in Vaught-Hemingway history (62,081), Tennessee led the Rebels 3-0 with less than six minutes remaining in the first half. The Rebels had gained 53 total yards and Bo had completed just 4 of 16 passes for 43 yards.

"But we always feel it's just a matter of time before the offense get things going," Bo said. "Nobody was panicking."

Finally, the offense rewarded the packed house on a third-and-4 at the Rebels' 33. Bo scrambled to his right and hit Sanders, who turned up the sideline when he saw his quarterback roll his way. That gain of 28 was followed by another pass to Sanders, this for 39 yards and a touchdown. Ole Miss had the lead, 7-3, with 5:08 left until halftime.

Golson picked off his sixth pass of the season on the Vols' next possession, returning it 18 yards to the Tennessee 35. That helped set up Walton's 7-yard touchdown run with 1:51 left to make it 14-3.

Wunderlich's 34-yard field goal with 2:04 left in the third quarter increased the lead to 17-3. Linebacker DeMarquis Gates forced a fumble on the kickoff and Marquis Haynes recovered.

On the first play following the turnover, Bo threw a 28-yard touchdown pass to Evan Engram on a corner route for a 24-3 lead.

It ended 34-3, with Wunderlich adding a 27-yard field goal and Dodson rushing 8 yards for a score. Ole Miss moved to 7-0 overall, 4-0 in the SEC.

One of the stats of the year in the SEC: Ole Miss held Tennessee to zero yards rushing — including minus-11 yards in the first half — and 191 yards overall.

The defense was improving every week, and Wommack was building depth at nearly every position. Haynes picked up 2 ½ sacks and led the team with 6 ½. Golson intercepted two more passes, giving him a seven for the season. Junior Mike Hilton also had a pick. The Rebels' were atop the nation in total interceptions with 15.

"You can tell from our play calling that we're comfortable as long as the defense is playing like they are," Freeze said. "We're very cautious at times. You have to figure if we can score 17 to 20 points, then we have a chance to win a lot of games."

• • •

During the press conference, I felt someone nudge me as he eased into the seat to my left.

It was 81-year-old James Meredith, who integrated the school in 1962. He was wearing his ever-present Ole Miss cap.

We shook hands.

"I don't guess they mind that I'm in here," he whispered. "I just wanted to hear the comments about the team."

"No, sir. I'm fairly positive nobody minds," I said.

. . .

Bo finished 13 of 28 for 199 yards, 2 touchdowns and no interceptions. And so much for him "chilling" on running the ball, as the coaches mentioned early in the week. He carried 17 times for 33 yards.

He hadn't committed a turnover in the Rebels' four SEC games.

At long last, Bo — and the Wallace family — could celebrate beating Tennessee.

"Their players were jawing at me some," Bo said. "I threw an incompletion, and one of them said, 'I can see why Tennessee didn't recruit you now.' I told him, 'Listen, I'm on the No. 3 team in the country and we're going to be 7-0 when this one is over. I think I'm pretty much over it.'"

After Bo's session with the press, I told him there was someone I wanted him to meet.

"Bo, this is Mr. James Meredith."

Bo's eyes widened.

"It's an honor to meet you," he said to Meredith as they shook hands.

Meredith smiled and nodded. "Y'all just keep on winning."

"Yes, sir," Bo said. "We're going to try."

"Mississippi will never be the same with what Ole Miss and Mississippi State have done," Meredith said. "No matter what happens the rest of the season, people will never look at us the way they used to. It's a tremendous positive for Mississippi."

Chapter 26

All anyone had to do was pay attention to LSU coach Les Miles' words.

Yes, he was known to clap awkwardly. He was known to nibble on stadium grass and mismanage the game clock in the fourth quarter. His white cap with the purple "LSU" across the front never seemed to settle onto his head just right. And his press conferences were famous for fiery moments and wacky comments.

"When I wake up in the morning and I turn that film on, it's like reading a book and it's exciting. I don't read books, but if I read books it would be like reading a book."

But Miles was a proven winner in the toughest conference in the country. In his previous nine seasons at LSU, his teams were 98-24 overall and 52-20 in league games.

Only twice had the Tigers failed to win at least 10 games.

He coached LSU to BCS national championships in 2007 and 2011. He did so using the philosophy learned while playing smash-mouth football for Coach Bo Schembechler at Michigan.

He believed in defense, a strong rushing attack and better-than-solid special teams.

So his response was noteworthy when "John from Gonzales" called and asked: "How are you going to attack the Ole Miss defense? They gave up zero yards rushing against Tennessee last week."

"We're not Tennessee," Miles said.

No, they weren't. Across the offensive line, including the tight end, LSU had four seniors and two juniors. The smallest was tight end Dillon Gordon at 6-foot-4, 295 pounds. Senior fullback Conner Neighbors was a 5-foot-11, 229-pounder who enjoyed his role of punishing linebackers and clearing the way for the tailbacks.

Three LSU backs already had at least 344 yards rushing. The leader was Leonard Fournette, a 6-foot-1, 230-pound freshman from St. Augustine, La. with 544 yards and seven touchdowns. He was considered the nation's top running back prospect of 2014.

Some analysts and media members believed the best way to attack Wommack's quick, slanting defense was to pound the football right at it.

Linebacker coach Tom Allen didn't agree: "We're big enough and we tackle well enough that we feel comfortable against their scheme," he said. Judging from Miles' response to the caller, we would find out come Saturday night in Tiger Stadium.

. . .

Freeze smiled as he recalled his first trip to Baton Rouge as a head coach in 2012, a 2:30 p.m. CBS game.

"I had a blast," he said. "That game will always stand out as one of the most enjoyable games I've coached in."

The Rebels lost, 41-35, when Odell Beckham returned a punt 89 yards for a score to tie the game midway of the fourth quarter. Jeremy Hill scored on a 1-yard run with 15 seconds left to avoid the upset.

"It was, at that point, a moral victory," Freeze said.

In his 11th start, Bo threw for 310 yards and two touchdowns. He ran for a 58-yard touchdown in the first quarter. He also threw three interceptions.

"We were young and really didn't realize what we were doing," Bo said. "We were out there just playing as hard as we could. It's fun to play down there. I'm looking forward to it."

In 2013, the Rebels shocked the sixth-ranked Tigers, 27-24. Senior Andrew Ritter kicked a 41-yard field goal with 2 seconds remaining to provide the winning margin.

It was a signature victory for Bo, who led a 13-play, 61-yard drive in the final 3:19 to set up the field goal. He picked up two crucial first downs running the ball and converted another third down with a 14-yard pass to James Logan.

The upset was a major statement for Freeze's program, especially considering his defense was missing five starters because of injuries. He lost at least two more defensive players during the game. Somehow, the Rebels persevered.

Five decades ago, this rivalry usually had national championship implications. It would again this season, with the Rebels 7-0 and 4-0 and ranked third. Twenty-third ranked LSU, 6-2 and 2-2, lost at home to Mississippi State and on the road 41-7 at Auburn.

LSU had drifted away from its grit and grind offense. It rushed just 36 times against Auburn, 35 times against State. The numbers may have been skewed because LSU trailed early in those games, forcing the Tigers to pass. But in wins over Florida and Kentucky the past two weeks, LSU rushed 108 times for 498 yards.

"They've gone back to their bread and butter," Freeze said. "Defensively, they're changing some things around that you haven't seen them do a lot of before. They've become very multiple the last two weeks, particularly last week. They're doing more odd fronts. They're giving you different looks in the back end, which you didn't get all of that in the past."

• • •

Bo seemed amped and confident the night before the game.

"We've got a good plan," he sad. "They've got really good athletes all over the field, but so do we."

I asked if he had read any of Miles' comments during the week.

"I haven't. What's he saying?"

"That they're not Tennessee," I said. "I think he believes they can line up and run the ball on y'all."

"No way," Bo said. "If he thinks they're going to line up and run it down our defense's throat, he's out of his mind. I'm not saying they won't get some yards. But our defense is physical. I don't know why people seem to think we have a finesse defense. I go against them all the time. I go against other teams. Our defense … nobody is just going to line up and run over them. I'll have to see it to believe it."

. . .

A crowd of 102,321 — tying the largest in Tiger Stadium history — was at full throttle for the 6:15 p.m. kickoff. Fowler and Herbstreit were again in the TV booth for ESPN.

It was apparent early that Miles was correct — this wasn't Tennessee the Rebel defense was facing. It was a desperate LSU team determined to win one the hard way — patient play calling, pounding the football, and passing when the Rebels least expected it.

The LSU players were also playing a little extra hard for their head coach. Miles' mother, Martha, had died at approximately 10 p.m. the night before. He informed the team during an emotional pregame meeting.

On its first possession, LSU moved from its 25 to the Ole Miss 12, but the running game accounted for only 17 yards. The key plays of the drive were passes by quarterback Anthony Jennings on consecutive plays — for 32 yards on third and 6 to Terrence Magee, and for 11 yards on first and 10 to Travin Dural.

But the Tigers came away with no points when Colby Delahoussaye missed a 28-yard field goal attempt.

After Ole Miss drove from its 20 to the LSU 30 and failed to convert on fourth-and-2, back the Tigers came.

A 40-yard pass on first-and-10 from Jennings to Fournette put the Tigers at the Rebel 20. The freshman rushed for 3 yards, then 14 more to the Ole Miss 3.

Jennings gave Fournette the ball again and he powered to the 1, but D.T. Shackelford stripped the ball and Prewitt recovered in the end zone for a touchback.

The Rebel offense needed only six plays to cover the 80 yards to the end zone.

Bo made a perfect throw down the left sideline — over true freshman Jamal Adams — into the hands of Walton, who appeared to score but replays showed he stepped out of bounds at the LSU 37.

No matter. Bo threw 27 yards to Treadwell on the next play, setting up first-and-goal at the 10.

Two incompletions — including a halfback pass by Jordan Wilkins — and a false start penalty left Ole Miss with a third and goal from the 15. But Bo connected for a touchdown to Core, who ran an out route from his slot position. Wunderlich's PAT made it 7-0 with 7 seconds left in the first quarter.

"We had a run called there, but I checked out of it," Bo said. "I knew I'd have Cody open on that because of the defense they were in."

Ole Miss had a great chance to extend the lead when Prewitt ripped the ball from Terrance Magee and C.J. Johnson recovered at the Ole Miss 48 early in the second quarter. Mathers rushed for 13 yards to the LSU 39. But penalties killed the drive. Sanders was called for illegal touching on a 17-yard reception — going out of bounds and being the first to touch the ball after coming back in — and tight end/H-back Nicholas Parker was flagged for holding on a 34-yard touchdown run by Mathers.

Gleeson punted and nailed the Tigers at the 6.

Miles' offense kept the ball for 17 plays and drove to the Ole Miss 4. Magee's 13-yard reception and 25-yard run on consecutive snaps were the keys to setting up Delahoussaye's 21-yard field goal with 2:47 left in the half.

Even though his Tigers trailed 7-3 at intermission, Miles seemed confident during an interview with ESPN's Heather Cox before heading to the locker room.

"If we play well on defense, which we are, and we can continue to run the football, we'll like the ending," Miles said.

• • •

Ole Miss' defense took a stand in the third quarter, limiting the Tigers to one first down and 22 yards rushing on 9 carries.

But the offense missed a great opportunity to add points when LSU's Jamie Keehn shanked a punt 22 yards, giving Ole Miss a first down at the Tigers' 34.

Mathers lost 2 yards. Bo lost 2 more when the Tigers' middle linebacker, Kendell Beckwith, came untouched on a blitz. On third and 14, Bo never had a chance to look downfield as Jermauria Rasco blew past Daronte Bouldin for a 5-yard sack. Bouldin, the redshirt freshman, was forced into his first meaningful playing time when Tunsil went out with a right bicep injury.

And in a game when every yard seemed to matter, an unsportsmanlike conduct call on Senquez Golson for spinning the ball after an interception meant the difference in Ole Miss starting at its 49 and the 34.

Golson spun it with little flair and no LSU defenders near him. Herbstreit questioned the penalty: "A little spin of the ball and you're going to give him 15 yards for that?"

More missed opportunities haunted the Rebels early in the fourth quarter. Bo had Treadwell and Sanders open for sizeable gains on back-to-back plays but his passes sailed high. The Tigers' relentless pass rush affected both throws.

Ole Miss got the ball right back. Hilton intercepted a second-down pass from Jennings at the Ole Miss 35 with 12:47 remaining.

On the first play after the turnover, Bo threw a strike to Sanders, who was running a post pattern and appeared to have a step on sophomore cornerback Tre'Davious White. But White showed a last-second burst and deflected the pass away.

"I had been begging them to call that play, and we almost hit it for a touchdown," Bo said. "I kept asking the coaches to call some shots down the field."

Walton ran for no gain, Bo threw to Sanders for 7, and Ole Miss was forced to punt again.

Bo and his offensive teammates were becoming more frustrated with every run for loss, every hurried throw, every open receiver missed. They could sense that one more touchdown would clinch the game, given the way the defense had played.

Gleeson was money again, punting to the LSU 8, and Hilton tackled White on the return for a 3-yard loss.

The Tigers took possession at the 5 with 11:06 left. They brought fresh legs with them.

Kenny Hilliard, a 6-foot, 230-pound senior tailback who had rushed for 353 yards and 6 touchdowns entering the game, had only three carries in the game so far — all on the previous drive.

Hilliard, the nephew of former LSU great running back Dalton Hilliard, was familiar with this scenario. He gained 93 of his 110 yards against Wisconsin in the fourth quarter of LSU's season opener and scored the winning touchdown on a 28-yard run.

Away he went: Hilliard for 2, for 18, and for 8. Melvin Jones rushed for 6, and Hilliard carried again for 16 to the Ole Miss 45.

Fournette ran for 5 and 2 yards, followed by a 2-yard plunge by Hilliard. That set up a fourth-and-1 at the 36.

On the third down play, inside linebacker D.T. Shackelford met Hilliard in the hole and began suffering leg cramps when the play was over. The sixth-year senior, wearing the red Chucky Mullins No. 38, had been a warrior against the Tigers' rugged inside running game. His 8 tackles hardly tell the story of Shackelford constantly taking on the fullback at the point of attack play after play.

Shackelford was listed at 6-foot-1, 247 pounds. His replacement, junior-college transfer Christian Russell, stood 6-foot, 235.

On the crucial fourth-and-1, LSU ran Hilliard off right guard. Russell stepped up and met the fullback, Neighbors, in the hole. But Neighbors, with a running start and leverage, cleared the way as Hilliard ran behind him. Rebel tackles Woodrow Hamilton and Lavon Hooks quickly closed the hole and tackled Hilliard.

By the length of the football on the ninth play of the drive, Hilliard got the first down with 6:56 remaining.

LSU's senior center Elliott Porter was shaken up while battling nose tackle Isaac Gross on Hilliard's run.

This set up one of the more interesting strategic calls of the game. Junior right guard Ethan Pocic moved to center. Evan Washington, who had handled the Tigers' "sixth man" role off the bench most of the season, took Pocic's place at right guard.

Instead of running left behind 325-pound All-America tackle La'el Collins, the Tigers ran Fournette behind Washington and fullback Melvin Jones for 22 yards to the Ole Miss 13.

Porter returned to center. Fournette rushed for 4 more yards and Serderius Bryant drew a flag for nearly ripping Fournette's facemask off the helmet.

First and goal, LSU, at the Ole Miss 3 with 5:55 left.

A blitzing Mike Hilton stopped Jones for no gain. The Tigers had ran the ball 12 consecutive times, and it looked like Jennings was handing it to Hilliard off left tackle on the 13th play. But an old football saying urges coaches to "run the play on second down that you are saving for third down."

Cam Cameron did just that. Jennings faked to Hilliard and bootlegged right. Tight end Logan Stokes faked a cut block on Golson, who was on the line of scrimmage. Golson stepped inside when Stokes pretended to block him, allowing Stokes to run past him toward the right corner of the end zone and snag a touchdown pass from Jennings.

It was the only catch Stokes — a senior transfer from Northeast Mississippi Community College in Booneville — made in his two years at LSU.

Delahoussaye's PAT put the Tigers ahead 10-7 with 5:10 remaining.

Ole Miss' undefeated season was in serious jeopardy.

• • •

Bo threw a 12-yard pass to Treadwell across the middle at the Ole Miss 44 to convert a third and 10. Walton lost a yard before Bo connected with Core for 9 yards.

On third and 2, Mathers ran left and cut up field. He appeared to easily have the first down, but Beckwith raced over and shoved Mathers to the ground like a playground bully. It left Ole Miss with a fourth and 1 at the LSU 47.

Bo quickly got the offense to the line and tried to sneak up the middle for the first down. But LSU got penetration up the middle and from outside. No gain. LSU took over with 1:44 remaining.

As the LSU defense celebrated with hugs and high-fives on the sideline, Ole Miss still had three timeouts. Hilliard rushed for 3 yards on three tries. A false start penalty also cost LSU 5 yards. Pack fielded the punt at the 25 and was tackled immediately.

With 1:19 left, Ole Miss had no timeouts and needed to get to the LSU 35 to give Wunderlich a chance at a tying field goal.

Bo scrambled for 2 and got up grabbing at his left calf, which was cramping. He called the play, and spotted Sanders open on a post pattern near midfield. We will never know how far Sanders might have run if the pass had found him. But again, Bo's throw sailed high and incomplete.

The Tigers applied pressure again with just four rushers. Bo stepped between them, ran right, and threw incomplete to Engram, who had it in his hands for an instant but couldn't hold it.

On fourth and 8, Bo read the blitz coming from the right side, and threw over the rushing linebacker to Pack on an out route for 12 yards and a first down at the 39.

Bo threw to Treadwell for 13 yards to the LSU 48 with 37 seconds left, followed by a pass that was batted down at the line.

On the next play, Bo looked down field, stepped up right, then spun out to his left. He let go of a pass down the left sideline where Ronald Martin intercepted it at the 11. But LSU's Jalen Mills was called for pass interference when he grabbed Adeboyejo, who was attempting to come back for the football.

"I intentionally underthrew that ball because I saw Quincy just behind Mills. If you allow the receiver to work back to the ball, you'll get a pass interference a lot of times, which is what happened," Bo said.

Ole Miss had a first down at the LSU 33, within Wunderlich's field goal range.

Bo took a shot with Pack down the right sideline, but Adams had great coverage and the ball fell incomplete.

It could have been a huge play. With Pack and Sanders lined up toward the boundary right, Sanders ran a delayed slant. Both defenders went with Pack, leaving Sanders all alone at the 25 with room to run but Bo had already released the ball toward Pack.

Fourteen seconds remained. Bo scrambled right and ran 8 yards before going out of bounds at the LSU 25 with 9 seconds left. It was a clutch, heady play that increased Wunderlich's odds.

Herbstreit praised Bo's performance on the final drive, saying "This young man made plays with the game on the line to give his special teams, the field goal kicker, a chance to tie it."

A rivalry with more peculiar stories than three books could hold was about to have another added to the list.

With the game clock stopped, the Ole Miss coaches called for the field goal with 22 seconds left on the play clock. The unit trotted out with little urgency, and as Wunderlich went through his ritual of stepping back and taking aim toward the goal posts, the play clock ticked to zero.

A 5-yard delay penalty turned the 42-yard field goal attempt into a 47-yarder.

Again, Wunderlich went through his ritual and awaited the snap.

Timeout, LSU.

Freeze welcomed the timeout because something was gnawing at him: Wunderlich preferred to kick between the middle of the field and the left hash. This kick would be from the right hash.

Bo was already preparing for overtime. "I had just told Quincy 'He's gonna make it,'" Bo said. "All of a sudden, I heard the coaches yelling 'Bo! Bo!'"

Freeze had decided to try and gain a few more yards and get the ball to the left hash.

Television cameras showed Freeze telling Bo what play to run, and Bo's facial expression was asking *"Do what?!?"*

Bo said on the phone: "It's probably best that I don't discuss that." But there was some obvious confusion.

At the snap, Bo rolled left with Rasco chasing him. The plan was to hit something in the flat and get out of bounds or throw the ball away. But Bo launched a pass toward the end zone where Core was double covered. The ball was underthrown, almost a carbon copy of the previous interception that resulted in pass interference.

No such luck this time. Safety Ronald Martin picked it off, took two steps, and fell to the turf with 2 seconds left.

LSU had upset the Rebels, 10-7, and spoiled their unbeaten run. Tiger fans raced onto the field to celebrate with their team, a sight Ole Miss fans would take some solace in later. When was the last time LSU considered a victory over Ole Miss worthy of storming the field?

It was a weird game. Or maybe we had forgotten what old-fashioned, slobber-knocker football looked like. But it had some strange numbers to go with it: LSU ran only three more plays than Ole Miss, yet possessed the ball for 12 minutes longer.

This was the sort of game that could splinter some teams or diminish the players' will. But Freeze's players had always reacted to a heartbreaking loss by playing even harder the next week.

In a difficult moment, with emotion boiling inside of him, Freeze showed great leadership while addressing the team immediately after the game. Some players hadn't bothered to take off their helmets, as if they couldn't believe the game was over.

"In life, it ain't always going our way," he told them. "I don't know anybody that's gonna go unscathed in this league. You ain't the first one to lose a game this year. We're gonna bounce back. Everything you want is still there. But, man, you have to handle the tough times just like you handle the good ones. That's life, and that's football and that's the way it is …

"Keep your head up. Make sure your words are what you want to be known for. Give them praise to the media. We will bounce back."

Facing the cameras and tape recorders, Freeze said: "We've been on the good side of these for seven weeks in a row now. This league is brutal. It's difficult each Saturday to win football games. Particularly when you may not play your best, and you suffer some injuries you're not used to having and you've got to play some other kids. That hasn't happened to us this year, but give LSU a ton of credit."

Bo finished 14 of 33 passing for 176 yards and also led the Rebels in rushing with 40 yards. But he realized he missed some crucial throws and reads in the fourth quarter, none greater than the last one. Dealing with that is part of being an SEC quarterback — turn the page and fight back or slink away.

I knew Bo would choose the former. He always had.

• • •

Bo told the media postgame that Tiger Stadium was "the craziest place I've ever played."

He was asked how it compared to A&M's Kyle Field. Bo shook his head and emphasized his original statement. "No comparison," he said. "Not even close."

When asked about the interception, Bo said: "I'm not going to talk about it. One on one. Threw it up."

Until that play, Bo had thrown 140 consecutive passes in SEC games without an interception. But in the "what have you done for me lately?" world of college football — and considering the magnitude of the loss — he was about to take a beating on social media, message boards, and radio talk shows.

• • •

A text alert sounded on my phone after midnight.

It was Bo. The team had just landed in Tupelo and was on buses headed for Oxford.

His message started with a positive thought, but changed five words later:

Bo: we're going to win out!!! we are playing not to lose!!! Had to bite my tongue in the presser. We can't run on first down, run on second down, then try to throw and let them tee off on my ass on third down… We've got to get a killer instinct.
Me: Hang in there. I know it's frustrating.

A few minutes later, Bo texted again.

Coach Freeze just came back here and talked to me… Said we're about to throw the heck out of it next week. I told him that's how we're going to win games and I'm going to carve Auburn up.

I stayed up and charted the first down play calls.

In the first half, Ole Miss was balanced: 5 rushes for 22 yards; 5 passes,

1 completion for 27 yards. Those figures do not include one trick play — a reverse to Core for 30 yards.

The second half was a different story: 8 rushes for zero yards; 2 passes, 1 completion, 6 yards.

Those second half statistics do not include the final drive when Ole Miss got the ball with 1:44 left on its 25 and was forced to throw on 7 of 9 snaps. The stats also do not include plays nullified by penalty.

Other than the first possession of the second half when LSU punted to the Ole Miss 2-yard line, the Rebels had decent field position: Their 34, 34, 35, 35 and 32.

After Bo completed just 5 of 15 passes for 105 yards in the first half and injuries mounted across an already-struggling offensive line in the second half, Freeze decided to put the game in his defense's hands and play high-percentage, field position football in the most hostile environment his players had ever experienced.

At the press conference earlier in the week, Freeze admitted the defense's dominant play had already made his play calling more conservative: "I know that if a team is struggling to move the ball and score points, I think I should be smart in how we attack."

In the first half, LSU outgained Ole Miss 243 to 206 and ran 9 plays inside the red zone (20-yard line and in). Still, the Tigers could only manage a 21-yard field goal. It was a valiant effort by the Rebel defenders, who had their manhood tested in Baton Rouge. Consider this: LSU ran 17 plays inside the red zone — or 24 percent of its 71 total plays — and scored 10 points. But LSU's defense — led by Beckwith, who for whatever reason didn't earn a starting spot until two weeks earlier — was fast, physical, and stingy as well.

Delahoussaye's second-quarter field goal turned out to be the margin of victory. Such is life on the tight wire that is SEC football.

Chapter 27

The Rebels were sore and beat up. They were angry and disappointed. And though it wasn't talked about publicly, the players were anxious.

History would be made during the 2014 season. For the first time, college football's power division would hold a four-team playoff during the bowl season. On Tuesday at 6:30 p.m. CDT, the first College Football Playoff poll was set to be revealed by a 13-member committee consisting of former players, coaches, administrators, journalists, and sitting athletic directors.

The final poll would be revealed Dec. 7, with the No. 1 team playing the No. 4 team in the Sugar Bowl, and the No. 2 and No. 3 teams meeting in the Rose Bowl on New Year's Day. The winners would play for the national championship January 12 in Arlington, Texas.

Ole Miss was curious to find out how the playoff committee viewed the tough loss at LSU. The Rebels had dropped from No. 3 to No. 7 in the AP poll and to No. 9 in the coaches' poll, which the players deemed harsh. Meanwhile, 5-1 Auburn — ranked No. 4 in both polls — was headed to Vaught-Hemingway Stadium for an ESPN prime time game. It was bringing an offense that was averaging 39.3 points per game and 6.91 yards per play. And while Ole Miss would again be tested against the run — Auburn's 281 yards per game were tops in the SEC — Wommack's defense would have its hands full in a multitude of ways.

Running back Cameron Artis-Payne was averaging 119 yards per game.

Dual-threat senior quarterback Nick Marshall could create game changing plays with his legs, and he had junior playmakers at receiver who could win their share of one-on-one battles. Duke Williams, 6-foot-2, 224 pounds, and Sammie Coates, 6-foot-2, 201 pounds. They had combined for 47 catches, 763 yards and 6 touchdowns.

Defensively, Auburn was talented up front and at linebacker but had given up 80 points in its last two SEC games, a loss at Mississippi State and a win over South Carolina.

• • •

Predictably, Freeze's Monday press conference featured plenty of questions about Bo's play at LSU.

Freeze took a stand for his quarterback.

"I would say this for our entire team, not just Bo," he said. "Our demeanor was a bit different in that environment. We let things get to us that have not bothered us earlier in the season. It seemed to rattle us a little bit. He missed some open guys. He also made some really good throws. I haven't noticed any mechanical things that are different."

Freeze pointed to the injuries across the offensive line and how inexperienced players weren't able to give Bo much time to throw.

He was asked about the interception at the end.

"I've got to coach and communicate with him better and make sure there's no doubt in his mind what we're trying to get accomplished," Freeze answered.

When Bo was questioned at the podium about his struggles in Baton Rouge, he didn't mince words: "We're staying in third and long so much … we have to get back to throwing the ball on first and second down and making plays like we did earlier in the season."

• • •

We talked later that Monday. Bo was still chapped they didn't mix in more first-down passes.

But he suddenly grew quiet. Finally, he said: "I'm more upset that I let that environment affect my emotions, letting the whole atmosphere get to me. I wasn't on my game. I was telling myself to stay calm, but I started getting real frustrated with the play calling. And I still think we should have taken more shots down the field.

"But I have to control my emotions better. Usually, I get hit a couple of times early, I'm good to go. But I could never settle in the other night. And I'm mad at myself for that."

Freeze talked to him Sunday about controlling his emotions. "He told me 'We're going to put the Auburn game in your hands. Don't turn it over. Just play like you had been before LSU.' And I told him I would."

He wanted to set the record straight about two incidents in Baton Rouge.

When Bo was holding up three fingers to defensive back Jalen Collins, he wasn't saying "We're No. 3 in the nation" as Fowler and Herbstreit had said on the telecast.

"I was telling him, 'For the third straight year, y'all have no depth on defense and it's going to cost y'all,'" Bo said. "And I was talking back and forth with Rasco, too. But it was all good. Rasco was saying, 'I swear, Bo, I love playing against you because you're going to always compete.' And I was telling him the same thing. It was just football, and it was all in fun."

Bo also took flak for going to the dressing room after the interception when 2 seconds remained on the clock.

"I thought the game was over," he said. "I walked around for a second, watched the replay on the jumbotron. They were celebrating in the end zone. So I headed in. When I got in the dressing room, the TV was on and I saw that the game was still going. So I headed back out, and that's when everybody started coming in. I didn't leave my team on the field intentionally."

In fact, the TV replay shows he wasn't the first to head to the locker room after the play. Others, including Treadwell, went in before him.

I asked Bo about the interception.

"I saw Laquon covered near the sideline," he said. "I thought Cody was one on one. That's why I threw it up."

"You didn't see the safety?" I asked.

"Naw. And that's totally on me," Bo said. "I have to see him. I have to know where he is. I felt terrible for everybody. Our defense had played their butts off … "

• • •

Just as Ole Miss was finishing practice Tuesday evening, the College Football Playoff poll was revealed on ESPN.

The committee still believed in Ole Miss, ranking the Rebels No. 4. State was No. 1, followed by Florida State and Auburn.

Rebel players didn't make too much of it when asked by the media. Auburn, they said, was the only thing on their minds. Not true, Bo said.

"Hell yeah, it was a big deal to still be ranked among the top four," Bo said. "It meant that we still controlled our own destiny. We win out, we go to the playoffs. It definitely gave us a lift."

It also meant that Saturday night in Vaught-Hemingway, the first unofficial playoff game would be played between No. 3 and No. 4. The loser could say goodbye to any reasonable hopes of making the playoffs.

Freeze got a lot of laughs during the mid-week SEC teleconference when asked what he thought when he heard Ole Miss was among the Top 4 in the first playoff poll ever: "My first reaction was that we will always be the answer to one of those AFLAC trivia questions … when the duck comes across the screen."

• • •

On my way to Oxford the night before the Auburn game, I stopped in Grenada to watch undefeated South Panola High School play. Coach Lance

Pogue and I are friends so I try to see the Tigers play every chance I get.

I texted Bo and told him it was so noisy and windy that I probably couldn't hear him if he called. So we agreed to text.

As undefeated South Panola came from behind to defeat Grenada on a cold, blustery night, I sat alone in the end zone bleachers during the fourth quarter and asked Bo about the Auburn game.

Me: What did you learn about your team the past six days?
Bo: That we're going to be resilient. Our focus this week has been what has me feeling so confident. It was no time for games. It was go about your business every single day and learn your shit because no one wants the feeling we had leaving Baton Rouge.
Me: Do you feel like the coaches will be more aggressive and let you attack Auburn?
Bo: Yep. We're gonna be as close to 50/50 as we can on first down. Have some shots in the game plan that I think we're going to try to take early.
Me: Where is Auburn strong? Where are they not so strong?
Bo: D-line is gonna be tough. Safeties are bad in space.
Me: D-Line as good as Alabama's?
Bo: As good if not a little better.
Me: Did the South Carolina tape help y'all?

[South Carolina put up 402 passing yards against Auburn the week before. Auburn won, 42-35.]

Bo: Yeah, we have a few things in that South Carolina gashed them with pretty good.
Me: What has your week been like?
Bo: Focused. A lot of talking to myself about not getting emotional, getting into a rhythm, slowing the game down in my mind when it starts getting fast.

Chapter 28

My eldest son once asked me the day after I had returned from covering a college football game as a sports writer: "Did it look as magical in person as it did on television?"

"It never does," I answered.

I was wrong.

On the first night of November, with clear skies and temperatures in the mid-40's and falling at kickoff, it was one of those moments that seemed to fall from a canvas as the two teams ran out of the tunnels. Helmets glistening. The third-largest crowd in Vaught-Hemingway history — 62,090 — screaming and swaying.

"It feels like the playoffs," ESPN announcer Brad Nessler observed.

And that is why television couldn't measure up this time. There was no way for the intensity and hope and *feel* inside the stadium could carry into viewers' living rooms.

Auburn was accustomed to big moments. It played for the 2013 BCS national championship 10 months ago at Pasadena, California's Rose Bowl and led by 18 late in the first half. Florida State rallied to win, 34-31.

On this night, the Tigers were crisp on the game's first possession, moving 73 yards in 8 snaps. Four plays covered 18 yards or more. Marshall ran up the middle for a 2-yard touchdown, and Auburn led 7-0 less than 3 minutes into the game.

Freeze and Werner showed their intentions on the Rebels' first play from scrimmage. From their 7-yard line on first down — where it would've been easy to play it safe — the coaches called a pass. Bo threw to Engram for 6 yards.

A possession later, Bo connected with Sanders for 18 yards to his 27-yard line on third and 9. Two more passes to Sanders covered 23 and 21 yards.

The 23-yarder came with Bo scrambling to his right and throwing on the run. Ole Miss moved 15 more yards when Sanders was hit out of bounds.

The 21-yard connection was the result of a great call. Bo faked a quarterback draw, then tossed the ball to Sanders over Auburn defensive back Robenson Therezie. Sanders stumbled at the 3.

On third-and-goal from the 4, Ole Miss lined up with Bo under center and three tight ends set right. All season it had been a pitch right to the running back out of that formation.

Not this time. Instead, Bo faked the pitch, then flicked the ball to Mathers racing left, to the wide side of the field. He outran one Auburn defender to the corner. Treadwell blocked the cornerback until Mathers reached the 5. Treadwell peeled back and blocked another defensive back with an angle on Mathers, who sidestepped the cornerback at the 3.

Touchdown. Ole Miss had tied it, 7-7, with 4 minutes left in the first quarter. Treadwell's effort drew a congratulatory visit from Freeze on the sideline.

Treadwell pulled another two-for-one later in the quarter. Bo scrambled left on first-and-15 from the Ole Miss 21 and found room down the sideline. Treadwell flattened a cornerback at the 38, then blocked another defender twice as Bo ran 59 yards to the 21. A facemask penalty on the play pushed the ball to the 10.

"Laquon Treadwell was unbelievable blocking on the perimeter," said analyst Todd Blackledge.

Ole Miss put pressure on the Auburn defense by alignment on the ensuing first-down, placing two receivers right, to the wide side of the field.

Walton was to the left of Bo, forcing Auburn to honor the run right. Bo knew he had favorable numbers to hit Treadwell on the quick screen left.

Treadwell caught it and raced to the end zone for a touchdown that put Ole Miss ahead 14-7 with 6:02 left in the first half. This time Treadwell was the beneficiary of great blocks from Engram on a safety, Walton on a cornerback, and left tackle Fahn Cooper and center Ben Still on another safety. Cooper was playing left tackle in place of Tunsil, who caught the coaches by surprise when he couldn't play after testing a partially torn bicep during warm-ups. Robert Conyers took Cooper's spot at right tackle. "And Ben Still played the whole game on one good wheel," Freeze marveled afterward.

Auburn took a shot on first down at its 43 with 1:03 left until halftime. Marshall let go of a long, arcing passing toward Coates, who ran a double-move post between Golson and Prewitt. Golson already had one pick in the game, his ninth of the season, and he had a bead on this one to at least knock it down.

Somehow, Golson missed when he went up and swatted at the ball. Coates caught it at the 4 and went in for the touchdown. The 57-yard pass pulled Auburn even with 1:24 left.

But Ole Miss didn't run out the clock and settle for a tie at the half. Bo ran for 13, then passed to Engram for 9. Three plays later, following a sack, Auburn was called for pass interference on Sanders, putting the Rebels at the Tigers' 44. Bo stepped up in the pocket and hit Core for 14 yards with 5 seconds left.

Wunderlich gave Ole Miss a 17-14 lead at the half with a 47-yard field goal — the same distance the kick at LSU would've been, but this one was spotted between the hashes.

Auburn outgained Ole Miss 237 to 200 through two quarters, but the Rebel defense settled in after allowing the first touchdown of the season in the first quarter.

Bo played with great composure.

"It seemed like the game was in slow motion," Bo explained later. "I knew what Auburn's defense was going to do before they did it. I knew where to go with the ball. The coaches had a great plan, and my linemen were playing their butts off.

"You always hear people like Michael Jordan talk about being in the zone and everything is going in. That's the feeling I had against Auburn. I felt like every pass was going to be completed."

He went to the dressing room with admirable stats: 13 completions in 18 attempts for 123 yards and a touchdown. On first down, Bo connected on 7 of 8 passes for 71 yards and a score. He also had the two runs for a combined 72 yards.

Treadwell had four catches for 32 yards, four key blocks and a touchdown.

"Keep doing what you're doing," was Freeze's message to his players at halftime.

• • •

A 23-yard reverse to Core jump-started the offense on the first play of the second half. Ole Miss moved to the Auburn 29 where Bo was stopped short on a fourth-and-1 run by sophomore defensive end Elijah Daniel, who was committed to Ole Miss in 2013 but flipped to Auburn just before signing day.

Wommack's defense forced a three-and-out on Auburn's first possession of the half, and a 20-yard punt gave the Rebels the ball at midfield.

They struck swiftly.

Bo hit Engram on a quick throw at the 44. Engram turned, split two defenders with a burst of speed and outraced junior corner Jonathon Jones to the end zone. Wunderlich's PAT gave Ole Miss a 24-14 lead with 10:36 left in the third quarter.

Treadwell running a simple out pattern on the same side drew defenders toward him and created the space for Engram to run.

Auburn answered with a 7-play, 73-yard drive. A 41-yard pass to Duke Williams and rushes by 212-pound senior Cameron Artis-Payne for 22, 11, and 2 yards set up Marshall's 2-yard touchdown run with 8:30 left in the third. Auburn had pulled to within 24-21.

The 41-yard pass to Williams rescued the Tigers on third-and-11. He came open when Chief Brown — called into duty with few practice snaps as he recovered from his ruptured Achilles — fell when Williams made his cut and ran a crossing route. Brown was forced to play when Trae Elston suffered a concussion in the first half.

Ole Miss punted after gaining one first down on the ensuing drive, and Wunderlich boomed a 58-yarder that was downed at the Auburn 4.

The Tigers went 96 yards in 11 plays to regain the lead. Payne rushed 25 yards on 3 carries. Marshall passed 14 yards to Coates and ran 19 yards to the Ole Miss 18. Two plays later, the Rebels' secondary blew its pass coverage. Marshall found Marcus Davis on a wheel route for a 17-yard touchdown with 1:59 left in the third. Auburn had the lead again, 28-24.

Ole Miss' defense looked tired. Perhaps the violent game in Baton Rouge one week ago was partly responsible. It was clearly missing Elston. And Auburn's tempo offense was creating problems.

"They were going so fast," Serderius Bryant said. "Before you know it, [Auburn] had run four plays in just a few seconds."

The offense needed to step up. On first down from the Ole Miss 20, Mathers took a handoff left, broke a tackle at the 33 and ran 34 yards to the Auburn 41. But he, too, took a blow to the head and left the field with a concussion.

Bo threw to Engram for 8, then to Treadwell for 6 for a first down. On the first play of the fourth quarter — a second-and-15 at the Auburn 32 — Bo passed to Engram on a seam route for 29 yards.

Bo scored on the next play, running 3 yards through the middle of the Auburn defense. Ole Miss had regained the lead, 31-28, with 14:26 remaining.

"For a kid that had so many problems in Baton Rouge last week, he has played brilliantly," Nessler said about Bo.

The unofficial playoff game was living up to its billing, and the only sure winner so far was ESPN, which was enjoying its highest-rated college football telecast so far in 2014.

. . .

For the fourth time in five possessions, going back to its final drive of the first half, Auburn scored a touchdown. Marshall led the Tigers 75 yards in 7 plays, the difference-maker a 41-yard completion to Coates, who won a jump ball with Golson at the Ole Miss 33.

Auburn overloaded the right side and Artis Payne scored on a 6-yard run to take the lead again, 35-31 with 10:23 left.

Walton returned the kickoff to the 18, and Bo went to work. With a linebacker running untouched toward him, Bo stood his ground and delivered a 24-yard strike to Sanders on a post route. Bo ran for 6, and with an Auburn rusher in his face, again, threw sidearm to Sanders on a stop route at the 38. The senior receiver broke two tackles and weaved his way for 22 yards to the Auburn 36.

He passed to Treadwell for 4 yards on a play that most receivers would've been stopped for no gain, threw an incompletion when he had to get rid of the ball, but connected with Treadwell for 17 on the following play.

Ole Miss had a first down at the Auburn 15, and Bo and Treadwell connected on a skinny post for another 9 yards.

"With the game on the line, [Treadwell] is the go-to guy for Bo Wallace," Blackledge said.

On second-and-1 at the 6, Bo started to throw a slant to Treadwell but the coverage was tight. He tucked the ball, avoided the pressure, and took off up the middle. He was grabbed by Elijah Daniel at the line of scrimmage and spun around. Bo landed on Daniel with his back to the goal line. Knowing he needed one yard for the first down, Bo began to blindly reach the ball forward with both hands. Defensive back Derrick Moncrief, a first-year transfer from Gulf Coast Community College in Perkinston, slapped it free.

Linebacker Kris Frost recovered.

"I was just competing, trying to get the first down," Bo said. "I knew I wasn't down, and it's just instinct to fight for another yard. If I make it, everybody is talking about what great effort I showed. It's just a situation where everything is happening fast and you're trying to help your team. But ball security is the No. 1 priority and I cost us there."

Marshall almost cost Auburn. On third and 5 from his 11, Marshall threw an out route to Coates. Golson jumped it and got a hand on it. Had the ball been a foot lower it would've been an almost sure touchdown for Ole Miss. Had Golson not touched it, it would've gone out of bounds and Auburn would've punted. But the ball bounced off Golson's hand and into Coates' arms at the 17. First down.

On a third-and-1, Marshall had his fullback open in the flat but threw it short and at the receiver's feet. Incomplete.

Redshirt freshman Jimmy Hutchinson's punt soared 52 yards. Pack returned it 10 yards, to the Ole Miss 33, and Auburn earned another personal foul penalty by hitting Pack out of bounds.

Ole Miss started at its 48 with 3:22 left and two timeouts to use. Its dreams of an SEC West title were on the line.

Walton lost a yard on a first down run. Bo scrambled right on the next play and threw toward Sanders near the sideline. The pass was incomplete but before the throw, Jonathan Mincy grabbed Sanders, who was about to race past him. The holding call gave Ole Miss a first down at the Auburn 43 with 2:31 left.

Bo threw for 9 yards to Core, who had motioned into the backfield, faked taking a handoff and kept running into the right flat.

A pitch right to Walton picked up 7 to the Auburn 27. A pass to Engram gained another 7 and he managed to get out of bounds and stop the clock.

On second and 3 at the Auburn 20, the Rebels ran the same play that Texas A&M beat them with in 2012 — and on the same end of the field. Engram, the inside receiver in a trips formation left, ran a corner route as the two outside receivers ran underneath patterns. Engram had a step on

Jonathan Ford at the goal line, but Bo's pass was barely overthrown.

That set up third and 3 at the Auburn 20 with 1:39 left.

Auburn sent five rushers at Bo, who quickly fired a pass left. Somehow, the ball managed to avoid the hands of a leaping Gimel President, a 6-foot-4 sophomore defensive end who did a good job of filling Bo's throwing lane.

Treadwell, who was lined up outside of Engram in a twins formation left, ran a straight path down the line of scrimmage as blockers set up a screen, which had produced a touchdown in the second quarter.

Treadwell was wide open. Ole Miss had more blockers than Auburn had defenders to that side, and the linebackers — Cassanova McKinzy and Kris Frost — had blitzed up the middle. Rod Taylor shielded Frost at the line of scrimmage on the opposite hash mark from Treadwell, and at the 23 McKinzy had to turn and look over his right shoulder to see Treadwell catch the ball.

Engram made a block. So did Still and Cooper. Treadwell avoided Montravius Adams, who dove for his ankles at the 12.

Treadwell was behind the defense at the 9, with only a hard-charging Frost, coming at an angle to Treadwell's right, with any chance of keeping him from scoring.

• • •

If only …

If only Treadwell's jersey had been a smidgen smaller

If only Frost had signed with Michigan out of Butler High School in Matthews, North Carolina, as many originally projected he would in 2011.

If only Treadwell wasn't 229 pounds and bull strong.

If only Frost hadn't hustled like a man who despised the thought of losing.

If only Engram or Still or Cooper had missed a block.

If only Gilmen President had deflected the ball at the line of scrimmage.

If only Bo hadn't thrown the perfect pass, which allowed him to catch the ball and head up field without hesitation.

If only ...

• • •

Treadwell saw Frost coming and offered a stiff-arm at the 5.

Frost got his hands on him at the 4 and was able to grab Treadwell's jersey just above the waist with his left hand.

Frost pulled hard and went "dead weight" on Treadwell at the 2.

Treadwell had the football 44 inches from putting Ole Miss ahead as he dragged Frost across the artificial surface.

At the 1, Frost slid into the back of Treadwell's leg, trapping the receiver's ankle beneath 240 pounds of linebacker.

Inside the 1, Treadwell's left leg snapped and his ankle was dislocated.

The ball wasn't knocked loose. It didn't slip out of his left hand. An overwhelming burst of pain caused him to let go of the ball 18 inches from breaking the plane of the goal line.

From the 2, Engram and McKinzy spotted the loose football lying in the end zone at the same instant. Both went for it.

Engram was forced to weave slightly around Frost. McKinzy had a clear path.

Their hands appeared to touch the ball at the same time, but McKinzy's straight-line momentum — plus a 30-pound weight advantage — proved to be the difference.

No touchdown. Auburn football. Auburn victory.

Ole Miss fans throughout Vaught-Hemingway celebrated. Most thought Treadwell had scored — the officials signaled touchdown — and didn't realize Treadwell had been injured.

But the touchdown soon went under official review, and players and members of Ole Miss' medical staff quickly gathered around Treadwell, who was still on the turf in the south end zone.

Vaught-Hemingway suddenly sounded like it does on a Wednesday evening in February.

Cheers from the visiting team and its fans soon broke the silence.

"... *the receiver lost possession of the ball prior to breaking the goal line, therefore it was a fumble ... ,"* announced referee Ken Williamson.

His words echoed throughout the stadium while Treadwell was carted off the field, tears pouring down his face. He heard them, too.

Bo stood in disbelief, as did most of his teammates.

Auburn ran three plays and punted, giving Ole Miss the ball at its 48 with 26 seconds left.

An incomplete pass. A dropped pass. And then a circus of a completion, two laterals, another forward pass ... and, finally, it was over.

Auburn 35, Ole Miss 31 in a game that, as time goes by, will become the modern-era 1959 Halloween night 7-3 loss at LSU. Just as they've spoken for five-plus decades of Billy Cannon's 89-yard, fourth-quarter punt return for a touchdown, fans will talk about where they were when Laquon Treadwell suffered a broken leg inches from a game-winning score against Auburn in the first year of the college football playoffs.

• • •

The only sounds in the Ole Miss dressing room were showers running, a few whispers and the clank of lockers closing. Players dressed hurriedly, some headed to the hospital to visit their fallen teammate, others wanting to get away from what had just happened.

Bo went around to his teammates, one by one, and quietly offered encouraging words. "We gotta keep going," he told them. "The season's not over. A lot can happen."

He spoke to a lot of empty eyes.

Bo holding Laquon Treadwell's hand after a gruesome injury in the Auburn game

. . .

Freeze was solemn as he met the media postgame.

"When you see your young men put so much into preparing for opportunities like we had tonight," he said. "you see the hurt that they go through. Whoever lost that game tonight was going to feel that way. It was a great college football game against two really good teams.

"It doesn't take away any of the sting that's in that locker room right now when you felt like you played well enough to win it. It's disappointing.

"The message to our team was very simple. Our character trait this week was adversity. We're staring it in the face a bit and that's life. Sometimes that's the way it goes. We have to be brothers right now as we stand together and get through a challenging time."

Bo appeared drained as he entered the team meeting room to talk with the press. He wore the team's standard gray Nike warm-up suit with a red t-shirt.

"It's tough. I think, you know, we beat 'em," he said, then shrugged. "That's football, though.

"That team," he said of Auburn. "It's crazy, you know, how things like that keep happening to them. But it's football. Life goes on. We'll come in next week and get ready."

He was asked about the team possibly being out of playoff contention.

"If [the committee is] really watching games, we can't drop far. We just lost a game by that far." He held his right thumb and index finger an inch apart. "I just watched a replay of 'Quon. We literally just lost a game by that much so I don't see how far they can drop us.

"Our season is still alive, we feel like … we're gonna keep fighting. Crazy things can happen."

A writer asked: "How good was Laquon tonight and how tough was that to see?"

"Phenomenal," Bo answered, and his voice began to crack. "He was really upset. It was tough to see."

Billy Watkins

. . .

As he left the press conference, I walked with him. I wasn't sure where we were headed.

Neither of us talked.

At the door of the dressing room, three or four managers were talking but went silent when they saw Bo. They nodded at him awkwardly, as if to say "Sorry." And they slowly walked away.

The dressing room was empty except for us.

He walked to his locker in the right corner, put down his backpack, turned to me and said, "Why does stuff like that have to happen?"

And he broke down.

He had kept it together for his teammates. He had held up for most of the press conference. But now the tears flowed.

We sat on the bench in front of his locker.

"As soon as I got down there, he was looking up at me," he said, still crying. "He said, 'I heard it pop. It's broke.' I was just trying to be there with him but the medical team was trying to keep people away.

"He reached up and grabbed my hand and kept telling me he loved me. I was telling him I loved him, too.

"It was just so hard seeing him laying there like that. It would be tough if it was any of our players. But Laquon is special. I promise you this, there aren't many players who are going to make me lose it at a press conference like I almost did tonight. But I hurt for him."

Texts were bombarding Bo's phone.

Bo scanned them. "Look," he said, handing me his phone. "It's from Archie." Archie told him to keep his head up and that he was proud of the way he played.

Lost in the shock of losing Treadwell was one of the greatest nights an Ole Miss quarterback ever had, especially considering what was at stake.

Bo completed 28 of 40 passes for 362 yards, 2 touchdowns, no interceptions. He led the team in rushing with 61 yards — that figure includes yards lost on sacks — and ran for a score.

Bo began asking me questions: Would they do surgery tonight? How long would he be in the hospital?

I told him I wasn't sure but that I had heard they wanted to do surgery as quickly as possible.

After about 20 minutes, he stood up and slipped his backpack on.

He looked at me and shook his head.

We walked out in silence.

"We'll talk," he said, as we exited the Manning Center.

He headed for his apartment, a reasonable walk from the stadium and workout facility.

I stopped and watched Bo disappear into the darkness alone.

Chapter 29

Freeze and his wife, Jill, went to the hospital early Sunday morning. The medical staff informed them that the surgery was successful, but that Treadwell faced a minimum fourth-month recovery period.

At the moment he was still trying to come to grips with missing the rest of the season — and with the football getting away from him at such a crucial point, no matter how painful the injury.

"As a competitor, in his mind, he let us down in some way," Freeze said. "Certainly, we don't feel that way. We're going to help him deal with all of that. He's a tremendous young man."

Treadwell's teammates, especially on offense, were taking the injury hard. Some of the young wide receivers — Pack, Dayall Harris, Sammy Epps — gathered at Bo's apartment into Sunday's wee hours.

"They were in shock," Bo said. "From their perspective, it was like watching Lebron James get an injury like that. That's how much he means to that group as an athlete and as a person. But the thing is, Laquon means so much to our offense in so many ways."

Statistics-wise, Treadwell caught a career-high 10 passes against Auburn for 103 yards and a touchdown. His blocks helped spring one touchdown and set up another.

He ended his sophomore season with 48 catches for 632 yards and 5 touchdowns.

"But his game goes so much deeper than statistics," Bo said. "He elevates everybody's play around him. Opposing defenses pay him so much attention, he helps the other receivers get open and his statistics don't reflect that part of his game. I'm anxious to see how people play us now. We've still got weapons — Vince, Evan, Cody Core, Quincy, Pack.

"Plus, Laquon was the guy who helped me get everybody lined up right. If one of the receivers on his side wasn't quite sure what to do on a play, Laquon would tell him real quick. If somebody wasn't lined up correctly on his side of the field, Laquon would fix it. Now, more and more of that is going to fall on me.

"And there is one other thing Laquon would do: I could put a ball up for him, and he might not be able to catch it but he would make dang sure the other team didn't catch it, either. I just don't know if any of the young guys have reached that point yet."

The Rebels would have one dress rehearsal to learn what it was like to play without Treadwell before closing the regular season with two SEC West Division games. The Presbyterian College Blue Hose, a member of the Big South Conference and located in Clinton, South Carolina, were set to visit Vaught-Hemingway Stadium on Saturday at 11 am.

"I love home games at 11 o'clock," Bo said. "The game will be over at about 2, and we'll have nearly a whole Saturday free. That's huge to the players because during the season we have very little free time."

At Sunday's workout, Bo began pushing the young receivers.

"I walked over to Core and said 'Well, you gonna make plays to help take up the slack?' I did that with most of them, and they're all eager to do it.

"I told all the young guys, 'If you don't know what to do on a play, just look at me and let me know. I'll tell you. But don't watch us snap the ball and you're not sure of what route to run because that affects everybody.'"

• • •

On Monday night, there was a knock at Bo's door.

"I opened it, and there was Laquon standing there on crutches and smiling," Bo said. "He hobbled past me talking 100 miles an hour. 'We can still win this thing. We need some things to go our way, but we're not out of it yet …'

"The dude had surgery two nights ago, and he's at my apartment trying to make sure I realize we still have a shot at the SEC West," Bo said. "He was calling himself 'Coach Treadwell' and telling me that he was gonna be at practice as much as possible to push those young receivers.

"I just smiled. It was awesome to see him doing good, and it will make a world of difference just having him around the rest of the offense."

• • •

Ole Miss may have lost to Auburn by inches, but it was also the team's second straight defeat after opening 7-0. On Tuesday, the Rebels slid eight spots in the College Football Playoff poll, all the way to 11th.

State remained at No. 1, followed by Florida State, Auburn, and Oregon. Alabama, with just the one loss, had climbed to No. 5.

I asked Bo if it bothered him to see State still unbeaten and No. 1. "Nope," he said, "because I know we still get to play them."

• • •

The night before the Rebels played Presbyterian, Bo said it had been a normal work week for him and the team.

"I've had a sinus infection and feel like crap, but we've gone through practice this week pretty much like we do for every opponent," he said. "I think the main thing for the offense is playing without Laquon for the first time, and all of us getting used to that feel. I admit, it's been weird at practice not having him out there running routes and catching balls."

I brought up the fact that he needed just 261 yards total offense to pass Eli for the school's career record. "I'd like to break it at home, and I'd like to have the football from the play I break it on," he said. "But we'll see how the game goes. When you're supposed to beat somebody pretty bad, sometimes you have a tendency to try too hard early in the game instead of just letting the game come to you. I'll try to not to press and just play ball."

• • •

Perhaps the most surprising thing about Ole Miss' 48-0 thrashing of an overmatched but feisty Presbyterian team was that 60,546 fans showed up for a game that started before noon.

It felt more like a glorified spring game, and some of the loudest cheers were aimed at Treadwell, who watched the games with his teammates on the sidelines and moved around using a three-wheel scooter.

Ole Miss led 14-0 after a quarter, 35-0 at halftime and 42-0 after three quarters. The offense gained 640 total yards — second most in school history — and rushed for 402 yards, the most since 1979.

Bo completed 11 of 15 passes for 140 yards, 2 touchdowns and also ran 9 yards for a touchdown. He was intercepted once.

He didn't play in the second half and missed breaking Eli's career total offense record by 106 yards.

"Coach Freeze asked me if I wanted to stay in the game and break it at home, and I said let's just get it next week," he said. "I appreciated him asking me."

Several receivers had outstanding games. Sanders caught 4 passes for 110 yards, including a 66-yard touchdown on the game's second play. Quincy Adeboyejo snagged five for 21 yards, and Derrick Jones — who had flip-flopped from receiver to defensive back the past two seasons — caught 5 passes, including a 31-yarder.

"I don't really know what we learned today, other than we had some guys who showed that they want to help take up the slack and maybe got some confidence going into these last two [regular season] games," Bo said.

Jordan Wilkins rushed for 171 yards and a touchdown on 10 carries.

Mark Dodson carried 3 times for 128 yards and 2 scores.

Defensively, Wommack was pumped that his unit got a shutout. Presbyterian gained just 156 total yards.

The best thing about the day, Freeze said, was that his team's locker room was "happy again."

The Rebels were able to enter an open date week with a victory. Their mission over the next 13 days: Get as healthy as possible for the road trip to Arkansas.

Bo dives for a touchdown against Presbyterian

Chapter 30

Bo spent the off week visiting friends in Nashville. Bryce and Baylee drove up from Pulaski to see him on Saturday.

They watched Alabama hand State its first loss, 25-20, in Tuscaloosa. Prescott was intercepted three times.

"It went just about how I figured it would," Bo said.

Bo used the off week to "work on my mechanics, make sure all my momentum is going forward when I throw instead of falling off to the left when my arm comes through," he said. "I felt like my mechanics were getting rusty."

I read him his numbers through 10 games: 190 completions in 297 attempts (64 percent), 2,554 yards, 22 touchdowns, 8 interceptions. In SEC games: 10 touchdowns, 1 interception.

"I'd like my percentage to be a little higher," he said, "but we haven't exactly been throwing a lot of bubble screens. Most of passes are 'read and throw' downfield. So I'm OK with it."

I asked if he thought Freeze would continue to be aggressive on first down, as he was against Auburn.

"I'm sure he will," Bo said. "You know, Coach Freeze has taken a lot of flak about his play calling — and I've been upset about it at times. I was really upset after the LSU game," Bo said. "But he's been an SEC head coach the same amount of games I've been an SEC quarterback. It's obvious I'm still learning or I wouldn't have let my emotions get away from me at LSU like I did.

"I'm sure Coach Freeze is still learning, too. This is not an easy league to play in, and it's dang sure not an easy league to coach in. But look where he has our program in its third year."

Bo also took some time to reflect on how quickly his senior year has nearly passed.

"I was watching film today, and I was like 'Two more games ... that's all I have left, not counting the bowl game.' It makes me so much more focused and determined to enjoy every minute the next two weeks. It's such a grind, but when you get to this point in my career you really embrace it."

• • •

Ole Miss gained one spot in the College Football Playoff poll after the win over Presbyterian, then two more spots during the off week. It stood at No. 8.

State fell to No. 4, and Alabama took over the No. 1 slot.

Auburn, now No. 14, dropped two straight after escaping Oxford — a three-point loss at home against Texas A&M and a 27-point loss at Georgia.

Ole Miss' dreams of winning the SEC West were still alive if it could win the last two and have Auburn upset Alabama in the Iron Bowl.

But the Rebels, who would be playing their first SEC game without Treadwell, knew they faced a tough task coming up Saturday in Fayetteville.

The Razorbacks were one of the most physical teams in the league, and they had lost some tough, tight games. They led Texas A&M 28-14 with a little more than 2 minutes left but fell in overtime 35-28. They lost 14-13 against Alabama and 17-10 at State.

But the Saturday before, second-year coach Bret Bielema enjoyed his first SEC victory in 14 tries and snapped the Razorbacks' 17-game conference losing streak.

They held LSU to 36 yards rushing and 123 total yards.

"I've said all year long that I felt like all seven teams in the SEC West were quality Top 25 teams," Freeze said. "Because of the schedule we play that won't be reflected in all of the polls, but I assure you this team is one of the better teams in the country. They don't give up many points. People don't rush the football on them. They shorten the game with their physical run game and their play passes off of it are extremely difficult to defend. They have talent at every position. They believe now not only that they can play close, but that they can win. We have a tall task ahead of us."

Plus, the forecast called for rain during the 2:30 p.m. CBS contest.

Rumors were also flying out of Gainesville, Florida after the firing of Gators' head coach Will Muschamp. Many thought Freeze was at the top of Florida's wish list.

Freeze refused to comment.

• • •

On a cold, gray, rainy day in Fayetteville, Ole Miss trailed 17-0 after Arkansas' first three possessions.

Things only got worse in the 30-0 rout.

On second and 10 at the Arkansas 31 with 14:14 left in the second quarter, Bo took the snap and looked downfield. The Arkansas linemen collapsed the pocket. Bo tried to step up but had nowhere to go.

Defensive end Darius Philon — a former three-star recruit out of Mobile who committed to Auburn and Alabama before finally settling on Arkansas — grabbed Bo and spun him around and to the ground.

Bo's foot and ankle were pinned beneath the 283-pound Hog as Bo fell backward. For good measure, 256-pound Brandon Lewis gave Bo a shove.

The ball came loose, and Arkansas recovered.

Bo crawled away from the pile in obvious pain. He got up and tried to walk to the sideline but managed only a few steps before dropping to the artificial turf and waiting for the medical staff.

"Very similar to the Treadwell injury," Danielson said as a replay was

Bo's foot and ankle pinned beneath 283-pound Darius Philon

shown. "That's exactly how I broke my ankle twice."

Bo limped to the locker room and missed two series. He received an injection and returned with 4:18 left in the half and Ole Miss taking possession at its 3.

He completed 3 of 5 passes for 69 yards to put Ole Miss at the Arkansas 13. But Bo's sixth throw was picked off in the end zone by Tevin Mitchel.

He broke Eli's record for career total offense on that drive, scrambling right and throwing 40 yards to Adeboyejo.

"What a courageous play by Bo Wallace," Danielson said. "He's barely on one foot."

He played the third quarter, unable to move much, and completed 7 of 13 for 113 yards. But he was intercepted in the end one again and this time Arkansas returned it 100 yards for a touchdown.

Danielson took Bo to task for that one, saying it was a "brutal" decision.

He threw one pass, a 3-yard completion to Wilkins, in the fourth quarter. After that, Bo and Freeze agreed it was time to let the younger guys play.

Despite the score and the offense committing six turnovers, Wommack's bunch never let up. After Arkansas drove 52 yards in three plays on its first possession, the defense played well. It held the Razorbacks, who lost their starting quarterback in the second quarter as well, to 89 total yards in the second half.

"I was concerned all week, for whatever reason, that we weren't locked in totally," Freeze said. "I think that showed in the beginning of the game. That's my fault, I've got to make sure our kids are [ready], but it just felt like a weird week for whatever reason.

"I really can't point to any just one thing … We saw some mistakes on practice film on things that we do that should not be mistakes. It was just a feeling I had. Again, I think our kids played hard to the end … we did some things that you can't do to be an elite team."

Because Bo returned to the game, few if any media members inquired about the severity of his injury. He didn't show for the postgame press conferences because the medical team was evaluating his ankle and foot.

I sent him a text, and he wrote back almost immediately.

Me: I'm headed to Oxford unless you tell me there is no need in me coming.

Bo: Naw, come on. I think it's bad.

Chapter 31

Bo underwent treatment at the Manning Center nearly all day Sunday.

We agreed to meet at Oby's restaurant at 6:30 p.m. for supper. He would have a friend drop him off.

It was wet and cold in Oxford, and the campus was eerily empty. Most students had headed home for Thanksgiving.

At 6:25, I found a vacant parking spot near the main entrance to the restaurant. I received a text from Bo that said simply: "Look up."

And there was Bo Wallace standing on the elevated entrance, leaning on crutches. He had on a dark warm-up suit and an Ole Miss cap turned backward.

He was smiling.

"You like to make these Egg Bowls dramatic, don't you?" I said as we shook hands.

As we headed toward the counter to order, I spotted former Rebel lineman Charlie Perkins, who was eating with his family. I stopped to talk with Perkins a few minutes. Bo ordered his food and got a table. I ordered and joined him.

"How is it?" I asked.

"I've got a big ass knot on the outside of my ankle," Bo said. "They're calling it a high ankle sprain. They'll give me an injection Tuesday or Wednesday that is supposed to help speed up the healing process.

"When it happened, I thought I was done. It was like slow motion. As soon as I got hit, even before I felt any pressure on my ankle, I was like 'Oh, shit.' Then when he pushed me back, I thought my leg was broken. But I could feel it in the bottom of my ankle, too, and I couldn't put any pressure on it.

"We went in and X-Rays showed there wasn't anything broken. They asked me if I wanted to take a [numbing] injection, and I told them 'yeah.' That first drive when I came back out and we went right down the field? I felt good then. But when I was warming up after halftime, I was like 'No way can I play.'

"And if the kids [Buchanan and Kincade] had been moving the ball or putting points up, I would've let them have it. But when we weren't, I couldn't just stand there. So I went back in. I couldn't move on it much.

"Finally, after I threw that first pass in the fourth quarter, I couldn't put any weight on it. I was hopping around, and that's when Coach Werner called down to Coach Freeze and said to get me out of there."

A young boy approached Bo and handed him a camouflage cap. "You sign this for me?" the boy asked.

"Yeah, I got ya," Bo said.

Warren Zevon's *Werewolves of London* played throughout the restaurant.

A middle-aged woman stopped by the table. "I just wanted to say I know y'all tried your hardest yesterday, and I wish y'all the best against Mississippi State," she said.

"Yes ma'am. Thank you."

A middle-aged man in overalls and a tractor supply cap also stopped.

"Ain't no way we would be where we are with this program right now if it wasn't for you," he told Bo.

"Thank you, sir. I really appreciate that."

When the man walked away, I said, "Have you noticed that nobody has even mentioned your ankle?"

"I don't think anybody knows how bad it is," he said.

"What are you going to do about your regular Monday press conference?"

"Show up and say whatever they tell me to about it," he said.

"What is the general consensus on whether you'll play or not?"

"The doctors don't think I will," Bo said. "I saw Coach Freeze and I said, 'I'll be ready to go Saturday.' He just smiled and said, 'You've got to.'"

"Have you watched State on tape yet?" I asked.

"Yeah. We can throw on them. I've just got to be mobile enough to move in the pocket. I can't just sit back there."

A woman walked up with a young boy. "Can you say hi to my son? He's a big fan and would like to have his picture taken with you."

"Sure. What's up, man? What's your name?" Bo asked him.

"Camp," the boy answered.

Bo shuffled his crutches out of the way and hobbled up to pose for the photo.

"Oh, no! Don't get up!" the woman said.

"Naw, it's good."

When he sat back down, I stared at him and shook my head.

"What?" he said grinning.

"The Bo Wallace that people think they know because they've seen you on TV and the Bo Wallace I have seen do that time and time again for kids … the gap between those two people is as wide as the Grand Canyon."

Bo laughed loudly, as if someone was tickling him.

We sat in silence for a couple of minutes.

"Any way to put into words what Saturday means to you?" I asked.

"I'm trying not to think about all that. I'm trying to keep my focus on getting well and giving myself the best chance I can to play," he said.

"Oh, by the way," he said suddenly. "We had a kick ass team meeting tonight."

• • •

It began with Freeze showing a side that few of the players had ever seen.

"I don't know whether to love on y'all or kick your butts," is how Freeze started his speech.

"He got us pretty good," Bo said. "And we needed it. I have never been beaten like we got beat yesterday. We didn't just get beat. We got dominated.

"Some of the guys spoke. D.T. and Cody and C.J. and Evan Engram. And it was like 'If you don't want to be here this week and you ain't gonna work, take your ass home for Thanksgiving.'

"They showed us a video of last year's game with them throwing up Landshark signs. Then they showed the part where Whitley came up behind me after I fumbled and head-butted me. C.J. went nuts. 'That's our quarterback they did that to! Nobody does that to our quarterback!'

"Things got pretty heated."

Bo addressed the team after that.

"I told them how much this game means to me, especially because of what happened last year, and how that game pushed me the whole off-season.

"Now here it is, and I'm just hoping by Wednesday or Thursday I can get some reps in practice."

• • •

For so much to be riding on the outcome of the Egg Bowl, it was a relatively quiet week.

Ole Miss dropped all the way to 19th in the CFP poll. After routing Vanderbilt, 51-0, State stayed at No. 4.

That meant State (10-1 overall, 6-1 in the SEC) would travel to Oxford with a legitimate shot at landing a spot in the four-team playoff. Coach Dan Mullen's squad was also trying to become the first in MSU history to win 11 games.

In its path was an Ole Miss team that had fallen to 8-3 and 4-3 and lost three straight SEC games.

But one statistic was hard to ignore: The visiting team had won only seven times since the game was moved in 1991 from Jackson to the schools' campus stadiums.

In 2009, Mullen's Bulldogs upset the Rebels in Starkville in his first year as head coach. He had fueled the rivalry by never uttering the words "Ole Miss" — at least publicly. He referred to MSU's in-state rival as The School Up North. The fans caught on and ate it up.

Gimmicky or not, State won 4 of the first 5 Egg Bowls under Mullen, including 31-23 in Oxford in 2010.

Freeze held serve at home in his first Egg Bowl as head coach, 41-24, in 2012. Bo threw 5 touchdown passes that night with a shoulder barely fit to pick up a pack of Skittles.

• • •

On Wednesday, I received my first text from Bo since Sunday:

Bo: I can't even take a pass drop.

I stared at the text. I read it again. And again.

It wasn't the message that shocked me, but rather the way it was worded. In all my time of talking with Bo Wallace — and that added up to hours and hours for this book — it was the first time I'd ever known him to use the words "I can't."

• • •

Later that day, I saw a Jackson TV station's Egg Bowl preview during its 6 p.m. newscast. The reporter had "great" news for Ole Miss fans.

"Bo Wallace's ankle is fine and he is good to go for Saturday's big game," she said.

Chapter 32

I talked with Bo about three hours before the 2:30 p.m. kickoff at Vaught-Hemingway. CBS's broadcast team of Lundquist, Danielson, and LaForce was in town again.

"I was able to go through some reps Thursday," he said. "I still can't move much. But I like the plan Coach Freeze and Coach Werner have put together. And I really believe my line is going to play their ass off for me. If they can give me just a little bit of time, we can hit some passes on them."

• • •

Yes, he had been thinking about the Egg Bowl scheduled for November 29, 2014. It would be his last game at Vaught-Hemingway Stadium. Senior Day. He couldn't imagine the emotion of walking out of the tunnel on game day for the final time. He thought of his mom.

"I know she'll be crying before the game," he said.

And Trina Wallace had been crying.

"Just about the whole morning," Trina said at the family's tailgating tent, located in front of Ventress Hall, the castle-like building constructed in 1889.

Several regulars from Pulaski had made the trip to see Bo's final home game. They were joined by Ole Miss fans from all over the South that had made a game-day habit of stopping by and visiting the Wallace family and having a Sun-Drop soda, which is bottled and headquartered in Pulaski. (For the record, Bo can't stand a Sun-Drop.)

"We've made a lot of friends here," she said. "And I'm sure we will keep coming back."

Bryce, who had just finished his eighth-grade season, hoped they would be tailgating before his games as quarterback at Ole Miss.

"He'll be better than me," Bo said on numerous occasions.

"There is no other place I'd want to go," Bryce said. "I don't even think I would visit anywhere else."

• • •

As Bo went out to get loose before the team warm-ups on a cloudy, 60-degree afternoon, several State coaches gathered on their sideline to study his mobility.

"I didn't give them a lot to look at," he said. "I just stood there and threw the ball."

Closer to game time, after receiving a numbing injection, Bo said it was working: "I can't feel the bottom of my right foot. I guess that's a good thing."

• • •

On Senior Day, Bo was one of the last to be called alphabetically. Trina was fighting back tears as he handed her the traditional rose. He hugged Baylee and shook hands with his dad and Bryce.

Just before that, Freeze had greeted him.

"These fans will never forget all the good things you've done for them," Freeze told him. "Go win this one, and they'll talk about it for years."

• • •

"Go win this one, and they'll talk about it for years,"
Freeze told Bo before the Egg Bowl

Ole Miss' offense and defense let their intentions be known early.

On the first play of the game, Bo threw deep to Sanders on a post pattern. Jamerson Love broke it up at the last split second, but "that really showed we were going to be loose, play to win, and put the pressure on them," Bo said.

Freeze even chose to go for it on fourth and 2 from the Rebels' 38. Liggins rushed for the first down, though the drive stalled six plays later.

Bo completed just 1 of 6 passes for 11 yards on the first possession. "I was sort of feeling my way, telling the coaches which passes I felt good on as far as movement goes," he said.

Throwing to the left side of the field was going to be difficult. Freeze adjusted his call sheet accordingly.

But his one completion said aplenty. With star defensive lineman Preston Smith bearing down on him, Bo stepped into a throw on third and 10 and connected with Core for 11 yards.

Danielson called it a "courageous throw."

It wouldn't be his last.

• • •

Defensively, Ole Miss allowed one first down on State's first possession — a 14-yard pass from Prescott to De'Runnya Wilson. But Prescott gained just 3 yards on 2 carries, and running back Josh Robinson had 2 yards on 2 carries.

Danielson was impressed and told viewers, "If Mississippi State is going to win this football game, they're going to beat Ole Miss at their best. This was a legitimate challenger for a national title until Laquon Treadwell fumbled that football and the air went out of this program. But they're ready to play today."

• • •

At practice that week, Freeze had told Walton that he was going to get the ball "until his tongue fell out."

Walton gained 6 on the first play of Ole Miss' second possession.

"He looked different to me," Bo said. "Jaylen always comes to play, but he seemed to have a little extra motivation … it was the way he took the handoff."

Bo passed to Core for 8, to Walton for 16, and to Sanders for 19. Walton ripped off a 14-yard run during the drive. Ole Miss had a first down at State's 17 when Bo saw his receivers covered and tried to throw the ball out the back of the end zone. He couldn't step into the pass, and it floated into the arms of State defensive back Taveze Calhoun in the end zone.

It was Bo's first interception in an SEC home game this season.

State lost 7 yards in three plays and had to punt.

Freeze had a play he felt certain would work on first down — Engram down the middle of the field. Bo found him for 46 yards to the 1-yard line.

On the next play, Bo faked a handoff and headed right. He bounced off senior linebacker Christian Holmes, spun and reached the ball across the goal line for a touchdown. Wunderlich's PAT made it 7-0 with 4 minutes left in the first quarter.

Bo went to each offensive lineman and gave them a "way to go" pat on the shoulder pads.

State cut it to 7-3 with a 45-yard field goal by Evan Sobiesk with 14:45 to go in the second quarter.

That's how it remained at halftime.

Already missing Treadwell, the Rebels also lost Sanders to a torn ACL in the second quarter. His knee buckled after catching a 30-yard pass near the sideline.

Freeze needed a receiver and a running back to step up in a big way.

Bo went to Engram at halftime and told him: "You're the one I'm going to. Get it done."

• • •

Bo rushed for the first touchdown in the Egg Bowl

State's offense finally got in sync midway of the third quarter and took the lead with a 9-play, 62-yard drive. Prescott rushed 1-yard for the touchdown.

That lead would last just more than a minute.

On first down from his 16, Bo passed 83 yards to Engram, who faked an out route that turned cornerback Will Redmond around. From the 1-yard line, Liggins scored on third and goal, leaping over the mass of players at the goal line. Ole Miss 14, State 10.

"I'd heard the State players saying 'Dive for their knees' when I was out there right before that, and I told Coach Freeze," Bo said. "He said, 'Do we call the jump?' and I told him we had to. That's why Liggins jumped over the pile."

State drove to the Ole Miss 18 but missed a 34-yard field goal with 6:43 left in the third.

Passes from Bo to Engram for 35 yards and Adeboyejo for 24 set up a 39-yard field goal by Wunderlich with 3:37 left in the third. Ole Miss led 17-10.

The Rebels' defense, as relentless as it had been all season, forced an ensuing three-and-out. Devon Bell nailed a 61-yard punt that gave Ole Miss the ball at its 9.

• • •

"He seemed to have a little extra motivation ... " Bo's observation of Walton in the first quarter.

It was a simple pitch right to Walton with an overload right, a play Ole Miss used time and again. State stuffed it.

Or so it seemed. Walton stopped, then headed left and saw a crease. He burst through it and was in the clear at the 12. He headed up the field in front of the visiting sideline. His feet kept passing yard lines ... only two Rebels had ever run past more on a single carry. Ninety-one yards, Walton raced, for a touchdown that put Ole Miss ahead 24-10 with 2:13 left in the third.

State made it a one-score game, 24-17, with a Prescott to Wilson 32-yard touchdown pass with 13:58 left in the game.

But two series later, after Wilkins ran 41 yards to the State 31, Freeze made the call of the game. Bo pitched to Wilkins going right, who found an alley and turned up field ... and then, just before reaching the line of scrimmage, threw the ball 31 yards to Core for a touchdown with 9:14 left in the game. Ole Miss led 31-17.

"We've had it in, but we needed to get the ball to the left hash mark, and we were able to do that on Jordan's run," Freeze said.

Asked how he was chosen to throw the halfback pass, Wilkins laughed: "I just don't suck as bad as the rest of the backs at passing."

State moved inside Ole Miss' 11 on two possessions late in the game but came away with no points.

And Bo Wallace, who finished last year's Egg Bowl with his face in the dirt in Starkville, was able to take two knees to finish the game.

Ole Miss 31, State 17.

• • •

Put to rest on this afternoon and early evening at Vaught-Hemingway Stadium were any notions that this annual rivalry game doesn't mean as much to Ole Miss as it does Mississippi State.

Ole Miss had lost three of its last four, its best receiver and one of the team's most popular players, and its playmaking inside linebacker Denzel Nkemdiche — both to broken legs.

It lost one week earlier 30-0 to a team that had won one of its last 18 SEC games.

The offensive line was an injured mess and allowed just one sack, and that came late in the fourth quarter when the game was already decided.

State had a multitude of reasons to play harder than Ole Miss, first and foremost a good shot at a playoff berth.

Yet Ole Miss played a step faster, and Freeze coached a step ahead of Mullen.

Jaylen Walton, who weighs 166 pounds, rushed for 148 yards — 12 shy of the combined total of Prescott, Josh Robinson, and Ashton Shumpert.

And the Ole Miss defense — No. 1 in the country at preventing teams from scoring — sacked Prescott three times and collectively had nine tackles behind the line of scrimmage for minus-27 yards.

State ran an astounding 84 plays to Ole Miss' 62, yet was outgained 532 to 445.

When everybody in Vaught-Hemingway knew the receiver Bo Wallace was aiming at first, Evan Engram was still able to get open, still able to catch 5 passes for 176 yards.

And then there was the quarterback, who couldn't put any pressure on his right ankle just three days earlier. A quarterback who was basically a stationary target for four quarters.

A quarterback who missed on five of his first six throws in the game and, yes, threw an interception.

But that quarterback, after his team lost the lead in the third quarter, threw what might have been his prettiest pass of the game — an 83-yarder to Engram down the middle of the field.

He leaves Ole Miss having won two of three Egg Bowls.

And in his final game at Vaught-Hemingway and on CBS' featured SEC game, Bo Wallace — on one leg — helped beat the best team in Mississippi State history.

"Bo has done so much for this football program," said C.J. Johnson, the junior defensive end who had 6 tackles and a sack. "We won two games the year before he got here. He has taken us to three straight bowl games, he's already been MVP in the first two — and we won both of them.

"I'm so proud of him. I honestly don't believe there is another player in that locker room who could take the criticism that he does and still go out and play productively on Saturday. I'm so happy for him … "

Johnson paused to gather himself.

"It's emotional talking about it," he said. "He comes out every week and plays through the criticism, through injuries, all the 'Good Bo, Bad Bo' stuff. And he still came to practice every single day and went to work.

"For him to play the way he did tonight with the ankle injury that he had … kudos to him, man.

"And State can say what they want. But that clip of Niko Whitley coming up behind Bo at the end of the game last year and hitting him while he was still on the ground … that's what I thought about all week."

• • •

After his meeting with the press, I asked Bo how it felt to get the Golden Egg trophy back in his hands.

"I haven't even touched it yet," he said. "It was being passed around, and it just never came my way. But I will."

He was exhausted after a week of little sleep, the waves of emotion, and then playing an SEC game without full mobility.

"I'm happy," he said. "But you know what I feel more than anything? Relieved. Because I knew people would remember me for whatever happened in this game. That may not be fair, but it's life. And it's the truth. I'm so relieved that we could pull together and win this game. I kept saying 'They still have to play us.' And I didn't mean that in a cocky way. I just thought our team was better than theirs, especially when we were at full strength. That's not taking anything away from them. It's just stating how I feel.

"And one thing I will always take away from this week is the fact that our training staff did everything possible to get me ready to play. Our head trainer, Pat [Jernigan], came up here every single night at 7:30 to treat my ankle — even on Thanksgiving. We had some great talks. Pat was with Tampa Bay in the NFL for 10 seasons and was part of their 2002 Super Bowl team. He told me some great stories as we sat around the Manning Center.

"Those are the kinds of memories that stick with you."

Epilogue

On the final play of his Ole Miss career, Bo Wallace scrambled for 4 yards on third and 13 in the 2014 New Year's Eve Peach Bowl at the Georgia Dome in Atlanta.

His ankle was no better than it had been against State, but he played — and kept playing into the fourth quarter — as TCU dominated the Rebels, 42-3. It was the first New Year's Six bowl, which was part of the new College Football Playoff. The matchup was selected by the playoff committee.

"We weren't expecting what we got today," Bo said that night, standing in the lounge of the team's hotel in downtown Atlanta with Chief Brown, Denzel Nkemdiche, and a group of friends from Pulaski and Nashville. "We thought they would be bummed about not making the playoffs, but they clearly weren't. They were pissed off, instead, and you have to hand it to them for that. When you think about it, we really did walk into the perfect storm for TCU."

No Treadwell or Sanders out wide. The offensive line disintegrated when Tunsil suffered a broken leg in the second quarter and Conyers suffered a knee injury that would require off-season surgery.

The Rebels managed 9 yards rushing and 129 total.

As great as the defense had been all season, TCU rolled for 423 total yards. Four of its five offensive touchdowns came on passes.

A season filled with a rollercoaster of highs and lows ended with a thud.

"It will take me a pretty good while to get over this one," he said. "We could've helped next year's team in the preseason rankings. That was important to me and the rest of the seniors."

He shrugged.

"Things don't always go the way you want them to, no matter how hard you try."

Ole Miss dropped to 9-4 and 19th in the final Associated Press poll. (There was no postseason CFP poll.) TCU, 12-1, finished No. 3.

There was a poignant moment in the relationship between coach and quarterback. With Ole Miss trailing 28-0 at halftime, an ESPN sideline reporter asked Freeze if he would consider replacing Bo, who threw three interceptions in the first half.

"I wouldn't do that to him, as much as he's done for this program," Freeze said.

• • •

A few things worth noting about the 2014 season and beyond:

The Rebels played the third-toughest schedule in the country, according to ESPN's Football Power Index, behind only UCLA and Auburn.

Ole Miss led the nation in scoring defense (16.0 points per game), placed fifth in interceptions (22) and tied for sixth-fewest touchdown passes allowed (12).

Senquez Golson, who finished second in the country with 10 interceptions, was named first-team All-America — Ole Miss' first consensus pick since Michael Oher in 2008.

Prewitt earned second-team All-America honors and was named first-team All-SEC, along with Golson and Robert Nkemdiche.

On offense, Tunsil and Engram were named first-team All-SEC.

Three of Ole Miss' victories came against teams that also played in New Year's Six games — Alabama, Boise State, and Mississippi State.

In early December, Freeze signed a new four-year contract with Ole

Miss that would pay him $4.3 million in 2015 — a $1.15 million raise. The contract made Freeze the fourth-highest paid coach in the SEC.

Ole Miss also announced in December a planned $175 million renovation of Vaught-Hemingway Stadium and the Manning Center.

In April, Golson was drafted in the second round by the Pittsburgh Steelers, the 56th selection overall.

Ole Miss headed into the 2015 season ranked 15th in the coaches' poll. Treadwell, Engram, and Tunsil were named to the first-team All-SEC preseason team. Robert Nkemdiche was named first-team on defense.

Though he didn't go through contact during spring practice, Treadwell appeared to have recovered nicely from his gruesome leg injury.

The Rebels' only major question entering the 2015 season: Who will succeed Bo Wallace?

• • •

Bo ended his career as the all-time school leader in total offense (10,478), most 300-yard passing games (11), passing efficiency (140.8) and yards per attempt (8.04). No player has ever taken more snaps as an Ole Miss quarterback (1,581).

Bo ended the 2014 season with 229 completions in 381 attempts (60.1 percent) for 3,194 yards, 22 touchdowns, 14 interceptions. Only two of his interceptions occurred after halftime. His 142.2 quarterback rating was fifth-best in the SEC and 34th nationally. Against Alabama and Auburn, Bo threw five touchdowns and no interceptions.

In his three years at Ole Miss, he completed 747 of 1,186 passes (63 percent) for 9,534 yards, 62 touchdowns, 41 interceptions. He also rushed 395 times for 944 yards and 19 touchdowns. His sophomore season, Bo also caught a 25-yard touchdown pass against Auburn.

He was talented enough to quarterback wins over perennial SEC powers Alabama, LSU, and Auburn, but he wasn't selected in the NFL draft.

He traveled to Kanas City for a two-day tryout with the Chiefs, along with several other quarterbacks. They signed none of them.

In June, Bo told me, "I don't understand why I didn't at least get into somebody's camp for more than two days and given a chance to show what I can do. But, really, I'm to the point now where if I don't play anymore football, I'm at peace with it."

He hadn't yet decided what he wanted to do for a career.

He said he would forever be indebted to Ole Miss and Hugh Freeze.

"It was my dream to play in the SEC," he said, "and they gave me that opportunity. I'll always be a Rebel. I'll always go to as many games as possible. I can see myself owning a place in Oxford one day and going back all the time.

"There is one thing I wish, and that is for the fans to stand up for their players more. Those players are their people. I know our team played hard for Rebel Nation. Stand behind them, even through the dark times. It means more than fans realize."

Asked what he will remember most about his career, Bo said: "Beating Alabama. The coaches. And the guys I was fortunate to play with. We were a close, close team. I was lucky to mature enough to open up and tell those guys I loved them and to feel their love in return.

"Few people get to experience that with a team. I've been fortunate in a whole lot of ways."

Acknowledgements

This book would not have been possible without Neil White of Nautilus Publishing in Oxford. Neil is a gifted writer and editor, and he believed in the book from the first time we discussed it. Neil, you are a true professional, and I will never forget your support, patience, guidance, and friendship throughout this project. I know I put you through the wringer. I hope the end result was worth it all.

I would like to thank Rick Cleveland, a former colleague and longtime friend, a terrific writer and a Mississippi treasure. His suggestions and encouragement were invaluable.

Thanks to my family: children Mandy, Todd, and Taylor; son-in-law, Kevin Cantrell; grandchildren Ryan and Campbell; stepfather Bubba Hailey; sister-in-law Polly; sister-in-law Pam, her husband Brian Quinn, and their precious daughter, Genevieve; and my soon-to-be daughter-in-law, Cobie.

Special thanks to my brother, W.G. Your constant encouragement and interest helped make this book come to fruition more than you will ever know. Always remember, there is nothing worth sharing like the love that let us share our name.

To my wife, Susan: Thank you for putting up with me, for your encouragement, and for believing in me. There is no book without you.

Thanks to the Wallace family: Bill, Trina, Baylee, and Bryce. You are "good folks" and I will always be indebted to y'all for sharing your stories — and your Sun-Drops — with me.

Most of all, thanks to Bo Wallace. As I wrote this book, it was astounding to look back and see how many times we talked beginning in December 2013. My wish is that through this book, the people who only know you as No. 14 in an Ole Miss uniform will come to know you as I did while reporting for this book. You're "a good dude" as Robert Ratliff likes to say. I will forever remember your loyalty to your coaches and teammates, your brutal honesty, your desire to win, and the trust you showed in me. It was one heck of a ride.

All mistakes in this book are the product of yours truly.

Billy Watkins